GHOSTS AND HAUNTS
FROM THE
APPALACHIAN FOOTHILLS

GHOSTS AND HAUNTS FROM THE APPALACHIAN FOOTHILLS

Stories and Legends

James V. Burchill, Linda J. Crider,
Peggy Kendrick, and Marcia Wright Bonner

RUTLEDGE HILL PRESS®
Nashville, Tennessee

Published in Nashville, Tennessee by Rutledge Hill Press®, 211 Seventh Avenue North, Nashville, Tennessee 37219.

Typography by Compass Communications, Inc., Nashville, Tennessee.

Library of Congress Cataloging-in-Publication Data

Ghosts and haunts from the Appalachian foothills : stories and
    legends / [edited by] James V. Burchitt . . . [et al.]
        p.   cm.
      ISBN 1-55853-253-6
      1. Ghosts—Georgia.   2. Haunted houses—Georgia.   3. Ghost
    stories, American—Georgia.   4. Ghosts—Appalachian Region,
    Southern.   5. Haunted houses—Appalachian Region, Southern.
    6. Ghost Stories, American—Appalachian Region, Southern.
    I. Burchill, James V., 1930–
    BF1472.U6G49   1993
    133.1'09758'2—dc20   93-30419
                                                                  CIP

Printed in the United States of America
      5 6 7 8 — 01 00 99 98

Dedicated to the people of southern Appalachia—past, present, and future—for keeping the old ghost stories and legends alive from one generation to another.

ACKNOWLEDGMENTS

Some names of places and persons have been changed in this collection of short stories revolving around the foothills of southern Appalachia.

Special Thanks To:

Big Ridge State Park Personnel
Sandi Nelson
Mable Aaron
Mary Teems
Martha Sanford
John Andrew
Ruth Roberts
Don, Matthew, & Cissy Crider
Ruth Jones
Maryann Herberman
Geraldine Barnes Kendrick
Granny Gravely
(the late) Evelyn Brawner

We give special thanks to the above persons for their help in making this book possible.

CONTENTS

INTRODUCTION

STRANGE, HOW ONE GHOST STORY TOLD or written leads to another and another until the mind is filled with haunts and hobgoblins. You can almost feel the dark as your skin prickles with goose bumps and fear grips you like a heavy hand.

Your heart hammers in your chest, yet you hungrily hang on to every word as if wanting to feed the fear, to relive the strange happening as it actually took place.

This was the situation First Draft Writers Group found themselves in during one of their regular weekly meetings.

First Draft Writers Group was formed in January 1987 out of the determination, frustration, and need for support of two people in rural North Georgia who only wanted to put words on paper to form sentences and to make paragraphs that went on to become stories.

Others who shared their desire were soon discovered, and now there are seven active members. To date, they are credited with 124 individual short story acceptances and publications and one disk book publication.

"We can write a book of ghost stories," Peggy Kendrick announced after all the members had read aloud true, scary stories about the area as told to them by family and friends.

"And," someone else added, "they are true."

The project was conceived, then carried out by four of the group's members. They gathered information and listened to strange tales told by local residents. Many of the stories were so old in their origin, research or verification was impossible. Only the storyteller could give the tale credence.

It seemed more natural for the old-timers to tell a strange tale of ghosts and lingering spirits, but many young people—trembling with the telling—also shared stories of unexplained mysteries that still gave goose bumps and nightmares.

The stories grew in number, along with the interest for a book enfolding all the tales under one cover.

With the words on paper, the group combined their stories, giving birth to a uniquely styled book that they lovingly christened *Ghosts and Haunts from the Appalachian Foothills*. This is First Draft Writers Group's first collaboration on a book. Working together were James V. Burchill, founder and head of the group, along with Linda J. Crider, Peggy Kendrick, and Marcia Wright Bonner, creative writers interested in keeping the old legends of southern Appalachia alive and preserved for tomorrow's writers and storytellers.

First Draft Writers Group takes great pleasure and pride in the written word. They also believe there are things that go bump in the night that cannot be explained, but are indeed there, just beyond sight and sound.

PROLOGUE

THE APPALACHIAN MOUNTAINS ARE AS old as time itself. The folklore and legends found here are as deeply rooted in the people as is the religion.

The gentle rising hills stand up and up, tall with trees wisping in gentle southern winds to touch a pale blue sky. The air is sweet and clear, the waters clean and cool, the soil dark and rich.

The people who first settled here were the Native Americans. Then others came—from Germany, England, Scotland, and Ireland.

They came to farm the rich soil, to mine the gold, copper, and other minerals from deep inside the earth, and to escape unbearable living conditions in other regions or lands—or perhaps they simply came because Appalachia was here, waiting and inviting.

With the arrival of the people came the beginnings of Appalachia's oral history, the storytelling. It was a way of sharing news and entertainment.

Before the introduction of modern technology, spoken words from neighboring farms and settlements were prized as they were told and retold from one person to the next. Strange stories of "haints" grew strong for visions and voices unexplained or happenings too horrible to understand.

Family stories, passed from one generation to the next, have changed little through the years in this region of the world's oldest mountains.

These stories are part of the Appalachian heritage, and having the tales of long ago told today often inspires a hunger for the history and lore that's always been here. The people and the stories of yesterday are part of us and reflect what we believe and how we see life today.

Without some effort at preservation, our southern Appalachian legends and folklore will be lost forever on the gentle southern winds—like the hardwood leaves after fall's first killing frost.

GHOSTS AND HAUNTS
FROM THE
APPALACHIAN FOOTHILLS

THE PLAY PRETTY

THE WADDELLS HAVE LIVED HERE IN THE foothills of Appalachia as far back as the census has been kept. A descendant, Mary Teems, has heard the strange stories passed down over the years. Sometimes she tells the strange tales told to her of long ago when her ancestors were young. Tales and mysterious things that happened to folks that couldn't be explained then or now.

"When Mama was just a little girl," she would begin, "her old maid, spinster aunt lived with them. There was three kids, Great Aunt Cynthia, and my grandparents. The house wasn't all that big, but Aunt Cynthia had her own room. She was a kindly old woman and everybody loved her. Of course, back then families were lots closer than they are now," Mary said, continuing on with her story.

One morning Aunt Cynthia came into the kitchen for breakfast and said, "You know, I have a play pretty that comes to visit me every night."

This got everybody's attention. Grandma, setting breakfast on the table said, "What kind of play pretty?"

"Well," said Aunt Cynthia, "it's just a little three-cornered light. It comes into my room every night and dances for me."

The kids all wanted to see the dancing light or "play pretty," as Aunt Cynthia called it.

"Okay," the elderly aunt said, eager for someone else to see the nightly visitor. "If it's okay with your mama, you can all sleep with me. One a night, of course, and see it. It's so pretty, just dancing around. Then it just goes away."

Grandma agreed and each child stayed for one night in Aunt Cynthia's room to witness the woman's claims.

Myrtle was the first to stay, then Pauline, and then it was Mama's turn. She said she got too tired and couldn't stay awake and snuggled down beneath the covers and was soon asleep. Sometime during the night Mama said Aunt Cynthia woke her up and said, "It's here, Mable. Look down at the foot of the bed."

Mama said she looked down and sure enough, there on the bottom of the old iron bedstead was a little three-cornered light dancing from one end to the other. She said she watched it for what seemed like a long time, and then it just went out.

A few days after all the kids had seen the "play pretty," Aunt Cynthia came into the kitchen for breakfast and, sitting down at the table, she said, "I know what the play pretty is now."

"What?" Grandma asked.

"Well, it came and danced again last night, all across the foot of the bed; then before it went out, it opened up there on the center of the bedstead bottom. I saw it, what was inside. It was a casket. It's my casket."

Mary took a deep breath and then continued, "Mama said Aunt Cynthia died just three days later."

THE PHANTOM DOG OF ELF HOUSE

FOR YEARS, ON DARK MOONLESS NIGHTS the teenagers in rural southern Appalachia talked about a haunted house down on the south side of Gilmer County, three-quarters of a mile off the main road. All the kids called it "Elf House." Supposedly the place got its name from the small stone structure the owner used to pick up and dispatch his mail.

It was said that the owner was a lawyer from New York or Chicago. He had no other family, and after his wife died he retired from his public job and moved here to the foothills of North Georgia to write. He found the mail service irregular, and often his prized manuscripts would not fit inside the regular mailbox and were left unprotected to face the elements of the season.

The rural-route mail carrier is said to have refused to make the three-quarter-mile trek up the rutted, red clay driveway to the house to make deliveries and pickups. So, after several months of ruined mail, the little stone Elf House was built to keep the writer's rejected works, along with any other written correspondence, until such time as he could break away from his obsessive writing to collect his mail.

The man was a recluse. Very few people ever saw him in the ten or so years he lived in the four-room, clapboard house. It was nestled deep in the woods and had few modern conveniences beyond electricity and indoor plumbing. He had no friends, nor did he want any. It was said the old man discouraged visitors and wanted no part of the social doings offered by the local churches or civic organizations.

The man was said to work in a tiny attic room above the regular main floor rooms. With the light on, he worked night and day, sure that one day he would write the world's greatest novel.

The old man did have a dog, or rather a dog was sometimes seen in the vicinity. It was a huge, black dog with a vicious bark. The beast boasted a very bad disposition when he encountered anyone about the property. He would bark and growl, rolling his lips to bare large, yellowed teeth. No one dared to confront the ill-tempered animal or its ill-mannered master, and soon the old man was left to his writing and forgotten by most of the townsfolk. The mailman never saw the writer-fellow either, but his mail was always picked up. Often there was mail to be collected by the postman from the little stone house to be sent on to some New York publishing house.

It has been told and retold that when the mail wasn't collected for about a week, the rural-route mail carrier contacted the county sheriff's department. It is said that when the sheriff and a couple of deputies investigated, they found the dog and the man both gone and the house empty. A single light was burning in the attic room.

A brief investigation turned up nothing: no body, no reports of a missing person, nothing. Therefore there was no crime, and no case was filed. But it is said the light continued to burn in the attic window, and it has been seen by many over the years who dared to venture onto the property near enough to see the window clearly.

A young man, John, and some friends decided they, too, would challenge the ghost of Elf House, and in the dark they drove down the country road to the little stone mail house. It was quite a test of courage. The driveway to the writer's house was overgrown with brambles, briars, and saplings amid potholes and boulders that looked as if they had slid or been pushed from higher ground above the narrow road.

John parked the car and along with four other young men braved the tangled underbrush. The house, deep in the woods, was deteriorating with age. No light burned in the attic window, nor could they see anything unusual in the dimness of their flashlights. They imagined they could see shadows looming and slinking about in the rooms with their falling-down walls. They had allowed their minds to scare them long before arriving, and so they became loud and boisterous to overcome their fears as they rambled about in the dark. Between the loud hoots and laughter John first heard the bark of a dog beyond the house, deeper in the woods. The sound was coming closer and becoming louder. It was the vicious growling bark of a very large dog.

"Let's get out of here!" John yelled and headed for the door. The others were right behind him. They ran, stumbled, and clawed their way through the vegetation in their path.

The dog was gaining on them, the growling and barking becoming so loud they knew they would be attacked. One of the group, who began searching for an escape from their attacker as he ran, saw a big tree up ahead and yelled to the others. All the boys climbed fast and furious to escape the dog with the death bark.

The five scared youths clung tight to the high branches as the barking echoed around and through

19

them. The dog was underneath the boys there in the tree, and it was real, not imagined. Someone flashed his light downward. The boys were terrified. There was nothing there, only the noise of barking and growling and the rustling movements of the underbrush.

"Where's the dog?" someone whispered.

"It's still there," someone else answered, noting the movement of the weeds and the continuous low, deep growl.

"There's nothing there," John said, straining to look carefully through the tree branches to the ground. "I swear. The weeds are moving and I hear it, but I don't see a dog."

The boys became quiet and still in the branches. After a time the barking and growling stopped and the weeds stopped rustling. Still scared out of their wits, the boys remained, holding tight to their high perches.

After what seemed a very long time, one of the boys broke off a limb and slid down the tree to the ground.

"If that dog wants his head mashed, just let him come on. I'm not going to stay in a tree all night," he said in a trembling, courageous put-on voice.

Nothing happened. Reluctantly the others slid to the ground. Quietly and quickly the group of teenagers made their way back to the car, scrambling inside and locking the doors and rolling up the windows. Their bravado returned, and laughingly each tried to joke about what they had just experienced. The boys trembled behind their brave talk, but each was thankful for the safety of the metal and glass that protected them from something they couldn't see. They wasted no time leaving the haunted Elf House with its phantom ghost dog.

"The dog was there," John said. "I swear. I heard it. We all did. It was so loud, and it was determined, too. And when we looked down under the tree, we could see the weeds and bushes moving as the dog paced back and forth, but the dog wasn't there. There was no dog."

A House with a Past

THE HOUSE STOOD BACK FROM THE ROAD, sheltered by tall oaks, with a view of the world from the front porch. It was not an imposing structure, just the dwelling of generations of farmers, but it had a long history.

The core of the house was a log cabin built before the Native Americans were driven from the area in the 1830s. As they grew more prosperous, the owners built on, obscuring the rustic with more refined materials.

When Sherman marched to the sea through Georgia he did not find the house. It escaped the rampant burning of war, but it did see tragedies of its own.

In the history of any place there is sadness as well as joy. People are born, they live, they die. In among all the living are weddings, birthdays, anniversaries. There are also arguments and conflicts. Intertwined in these events are emotions.

Speculation has been made that a house haunted is a house that retains energy and emotion from past events. This house could not escape that fate, nor could it hide its hauntings from those who later dwelt there.

In the summer, not so many years ago, a family named Owens came from the Atlanta area to escape the intensity of the city. They sought the imagined tranquility of a rural area and were excited when their real estate agent showed them the old farmhouse. It needed many improvements, but they were looking forward to that.

They wanted to make the house their own, to change it to their liking, to bond with it as if they had built it. To this end they made elaborate plans and started their work almost immediately.

First, the kitchen had to go. It was antiquated, even ugly. They started ripping things out, never realizing that at one time the things they ripped out had been someone's idea of a dream. Pine cabinets, Formica tops, large enamel range, stainless steel sink—all taken to the dump, gone. That was when it started.

At first it was things misplaced. Tools, clothes, books. The new residents hardly noticed until they went looking for these possessions and found them in odd places. Screwdrivers were always found driven among the roots of an oak in the backyard. Clothes would be in the back of the closet done up in tight balls and shoved in a corner. Books, for some reason, ended up in the barn loft.

At first the family was charmed. They felt honored to have a ghost in the house. The tools were still usable, the clothes could be ironed, and the barn loft was an excellent place to read. But the fire in the smokehouse changed their minds.

The parents suspected one of the children. Children like to play with matches, and they rarely own up to guilt. Of course the children denied any knowledge of the fire in the old smokehouse. They did not want to be punished, the parents thought. The second fire was more perplexing. When this fire started, the children were at the public swimming pool in the county seat.

The shed that burned was one they had not explored because of the weeds and a fear of snakes. The shed and

its contents were burned to ash and lost to time. If anything valuable had been inside, the family would never
know.

School began about the time the kitchen was finished, and not only did the children start classes but the
mother did as well. She traveled south to a small two-year
college with a good horticulture program. Next year, she
hoped, they would have a garden and flowers to envy.

Left alone, the man went to work on the only bathroom in the house. He rented a portable toilet and ripped
out the bathroom to the bare walls. As usual, there were
misplaced tools and even a small fire in the barn. Despite
this, the bathroom was finished in time for a Halloween
party.

New friends and old friends came to the party. In all,
about a hundred people drove up the jack o'lantern-lined
driveway and parked in a field beside the house. The
festivities were not to be grand, but they were to be traditional.

There were games, apple bobbing being the chief one
and the most amusing. They had a hay ride in a large
wagon pulled by a tractor. Among the guests was a local
man renowned for his ghost stories.

The Owens family told those gathered about the
strange happenings on the place, and the local man confirmed them with a few of his own tales about the house.
He claimed there was not just one ghost but several.

When the evening ended, the local man was one of
the last to go. He exchanged thanks with the family and
said an odd thing before he left. "You'll start seeing them
soon," he said, and the family nervously laughed this off.

Having pranks played on you by unseen ghosts was
one thing, but actually seeing those pranksters? That was
something they did not look forward to. Unfortunately,
the sightings started to happen all too soon.

Left alone, Mr. Owens worked inside and outside the

house, but he began to feel he was not really alone. He suspected that someone was watching him, and he did not like the feeling. It was like a subtle invasion of privacy.

When he got fed up with his suspicions, Mr. Owens started looking for a logical explanation. He suspected one of his neighbors, but since he never saw anything, except sometimes out of the corner of his eye, Mr. Owens decided he was letting his imagination run wild. The woman in calico changed his mind.

He first saw her near the barn, and at the time he thought she was one of the neighbors come to visit or just taking a walk. When he waved to her, she just stared. Feeling embarrassed, he went back to chopping wood. Looking up again, he found her gone.

The second time he was in the kitchen enjoying a midmorning coffee break while reading the gardening section of the Sunday paper. He happened to glance out the window as he was putting his mug down on the table when he saw her once again. She was standing out by the barn, but this time she was not alone.

She had a child with her. A boy. Getting a better look at her this time, Mr. Owens saw she had wispy blond hair. The boy's was almost the same, and he wore overalls without a shirt or shoes. She wore a faded dress that reached to her ankles. By the time he reached the back porch, they were gone.

After that he saw them all the time. He never saw them arrive, and he never saw them leave. He would just look up, and they would be standing there, watching him. No one else saw them until his sister arrived for Thanksgiving.

The moment Laura got out of her car, she sensed something out of the ordinary about the old farm. She spent the first hour walking around with the family exploring this new place. When they sat down in the living room to rest before dinner, she asked them if the farm was haunted.

Mr. Owens said yes but did not tell Laura his experiences. He wanted to hear her impressions before he told her what had happened to him. Those impressions were very similar to his own.

"I think they're brother and sister," she said of the woman and boy he kept seeing. "As for the others . . ."

"Others?" Mrs. Owens asked, rather daunted by the word.

"The older boy," Laura said. "He was around that shed, the smokehouse. He smells of smoke. And there's the old woman in the kitchen. She doesn't like the changes you've made. She likes to hide things. She thinks people are going to rob her. I don't think she's quite right. In the head."

"Is there anyone else?" her brother asked.

"I saw a marmalade cat," Laura replied.

"Where?"

"It was sitting among the roots of that oak tree in the back yard."

"We don't have a cat."

"I didn't think so. Real cats don't usually vanish into thin air."

After that the Owens saw the cat often—fleeting glimpses from the corners of their eyes. There were even a few more small fires, and if anything went missing they looked to the roots of the oak tree or in the barn loft. With winter the woman and boy stopped appearing. Perhaps it was too cold for them. In the spring Mr. Owens saw them again, and a neighbor helping him build a fence saw them as well. Moreover, the neighbor recognized them.

"That's Emmy and Joshua," he explained. "They died of the influenza. I was just a boy then, but I remember them."

Mr. Owens related his sister's impressions about the

other ghosts, and the man knew at least the human ones. The older boy was Mark. He had died, suffocated in the smokehouse after he was locked in there by some other boys. The old woman was Nancy. She died at 98, telling everyone who would listen that people were trying to rob her.

It is best to make peace with your ghosts, both real and imagined. With peace comes acceptance, with acceptance contentment, and you realize there are some things you cannot change. With this the family realized there was an order to the old farm. They realized some things should not be altered. They modified their own plans to include those of past generations.

Today the farm is still haunted by people and events of the past, but the Owens family has learned to live with them. Emmy and Joshua still come to watch the father work, but now that the house is fully renovated Nancy bothers them only occasionally. The cat is seen now and again, but it could be a real cat that strayed onto the property. The only one gone is Mark. He left after the family tore down the old smokehouse and planted a flower garden where he died.

GHOST WAGON

FOLKS IN THE WESTERN SECTION OF Gilmer County, Georgia, namely the Jones and Stamey families, tell of a ghost wagon. Most members of these parties have heard the wagon coming down the old logging road and a man screaming, "Lucy!"

The tale is said to have taken place in the 1930s during the Great Depression. Folks didn't have much back then, but they did their best.

The beginning of the ghost wagon story starts innocently enough. Homer and Lucy were to be married two weeks from the following Sunday. They were young and in love and had bought a tract of land in the western area of Gilmer County. Their plan was to clear a section for their cabin. Kinfolks and church members would then throw up their cabin.

The property was heavily wooded but had an old logging road running through it. On that fateful day, Homer, with Lucy cheering him on, was cutting down trees just off the old logging road.

"Now you stand over there, Lucy, honey," said Homer. "This old tree is going to fall away from you."

Lucy did as she was bidden. Her lively smile would

have told anyone how happy she was—she and Homer forever.

Homer gave the massive oak one more cut. It creaked, then as if the oak tree knew it was dying, screamed and fell on Lucy.

Homer's cry could be heard throughout the valley.

"Lucy!" He rushed to her side and hacked at the branches, crying all the time, "Lucy!"

With almost superhuman strength, he rolled the large tree trunk off his beloved.

"I'll get you to the doctor. Don't worry Lucy, honey. I'll get you help."

Homer gently laid Lucy in the back of their wagon and started down the old logging road.

"Don't worry," moaned Homer. "If it takes forever, I'll get you help."

Halfway down the logging road, Homer stopped the wagon and checked on his only love. Lucy was still, her once-bright eyes closed. She was gray, and Homer knew without a doubt his Lucy was gone.

Racked with grief, Homer stumbled to the front of the wagon, reached under the seat, and brought out his shotgun. No one heard the blast. But today, many years later, folks in western Gilmer County can still hear an old wagon rolling down the logging road. They also hear a scream, "Lucy!" But the wagon never completes its tragic journey.

DEVIL'S VISION

IT HAS BEEN TOLD AND RETOLD OVER THE years that a strange woman once lived on the eastern side of the Tennessee border. She saw things and spoke of things happening to the people living in the county, things people didn't want seen or spoken of. When the old woman was confronted, she'd just laugh and rub her hands together briskly as if she knew more than she told.

It's said that when the sun began to lean toward the west, she would take a large, old-fashioned, round metal-screen wire flour sifter from a high shelf in her kitchen. She would then hobble her way to the front porch of her small, log house where she would sit in a high-backed rocker.

She would rock back and forth on the creaky porch floor with the flour sifter resting on her lap.

When the sun began to lay low, barely hanging onto the sky—just before it fell behind the dark mountains—the old woman would hold the flour sifter up before her face and gaze into the little squares of the metal screen. She would rock and laugh and stare as if in some kind of trance. This was a daily ritual with her, and once a passerby, seeing the old woman practicing such unusual behavior, walked up on the porch. He asked what she was doing.

"I just look through my flour sifter here," she said, "and I can see and hear what everybody in the county is doing."

The questioning passerby looked through the flour sifter held by the old woman as she continued to rock, stare, and laugh. He saw nothing. He heard nothing.

"I don't see or hear anything," he said. "How is it that you can see all you say you see?"

"If you sell your soul to the Devil, you can see and hear anything you want," the old woman said as she continued to rock and stare through the tiny squares in the round, old-fashioned sifter.

A Brush of Cool

His name was Archie. Tory became aware of his existence when she was about fifteen. She never saw him but rather felt his presence, somewhat knowing that she was being protected or maybe warned of some imminent danger or crisis close at hand.

Sometimes she saw his warnings as a flash of bright blue light caught from the corner of her eye. Other times it was a cool brush against her cheek or her arm, but she always knew it was Archie.

There were times when he was gone from her life, times that no warnings of crisis were given and she would call to him, "Archie, where were you when I needed you? Where are you now?"

A hush would follow. Then the brush of coolness would touch her or a flash of light would glimmer, and she would know he was still there somewhere, watching over her. Her life continued and deepened, filled with career, husband, and children.

Tory never mentioned her protector to anyone, only smiled and gave a silent, "Thank you, Archie," when he warned her of state patrols with radar and speed traps around a curve in the road, or let her know to ready herself for a troublesome day.

After some thirty years, Archie became a bit more bold and began to interrupt phone calls to warn that bad news would soon come across the wires.

"I'm not prepared," she said once, trying to ignore the high-pitched squeal on the telephone line as she talked with Vince, her writing partner. She couldn't ignore the noise when it sounded three more times and the phone went dead—blank of everything but the high-pitched squeal—and she felt a brush of cool against her cheek.

"Okay, Archie," she said. "It's evident you're not going to give up. What do I need to do now? Dress? Pack a bag? Cook? It's your call." Before she could ask another question, the phone rang. Tory answered, "Hello."

It was her sister Lee, a nurse at the local hospital.

"Tory. Call Uncle Ray. Ben is really bad sick, and Mother is in a panic. Do whatever you have to do. I'll look after things here on this end, and I'll get back to you."

"Okay," Tory answered.

"Are you okay?" Lee asked. "You sound almost too calm."

"You could say I've been waiting for your call," Tory replied.

"You've always been weird," Lee commented. "I'm being paged. I'll get back to you soon. Call Uncle Ray."

"I will," she answered, hanging up the phone.

"Three times you've done this now in the past two weeks, Archie. First it was Uncle Marvin's death, then it was my friend Charles. Always, you do this and in less than twenty-four hours, the call comes announcing yet another crisis," Tory said, punching the telephone numbers. "Now someone else knows about you. But don't go. I really do need you."

As the phone rang on the other end, a coolness brushed her brow and she felt somewhat comforted, knowing she had Archie, her guardian angel, there to give her warning, a bit of time to still herself for whatever trouble awaited her. As long as Tory could feel the brush of cool, see the slight flash of bright blue light, or hear the high-pitched squeals on her telephone line, she knew she would never be truly alone, and she smiled a sad smile and waited for Uncle Ray to answer his telephone.

Silent Sounds

Annie Trotter, a young woman of nineteen, lived with her grandparents in Hickory Ridge, Virginia. She was a quiet girl who didn't socialize much, according to those who knew her. She was beautiful, with chestnut hair and silky, smooth skin. People always commented on her amber-colored eyes, saying things like, "Bet you could look right into the soul of a body," and "Do you see the same things I do when you look at something?"

But it has been told that her vision was not her most unusual characteristic—it was her hearing. She could hear things all over the country as they were happening.

"It's 'cause of that pa of her'n," Natti Ames, the girl's grandma would say whenever anyone brought it up. "Told Roxie's pa, the day before he married her, he were a gypsy, he did. But I always figured he was some kinda magic man. Didn't stay around long enough to know fer sure. Annie's ma, my girl, Roxie, died after the birthing, and her pa just up and left. Ain't nobody seen or heard tell of him since." The old woman would always sigh then and continue, "But I figure she got this hearing gift from him. Ain't nobody on the other side of the family got any special gifts."

One hot July morning, it was said, a traveling preacher dropped by the Ames place to invite the folks to the next week's protracted tent meeting at the county fairgrounds.

Natti gave the preacher a dipper of cool water. As the man drank, he and the old woman discussed the weather, names of the neighbors, the Scriptures, and general small talk. It was told that while the two talked back and forth, Annie heard a roaring. It grew so loud she could no longer hear the voices of the preacher and her grandma, even though she could see their lips move and their expressions change.

The roaring continued to grow, then the girl heard an explosion. With the noise of the explosion dying, all became quiet, and the voices of the preacher and her grandma returned.

Natti, noting the girl's expression asked, "What's wrong, girl? What you hearing now?"

The girl remained silent, not wanting to draw any attention to herself.

An hour later, the radio news broadcast that an airplane had crashed, killing a United States senator.

The girl sighed, then shivered, upon hearing the announcement. She knew she had heard the crash as it had happened. She cursed, and as tears rimmed her amber-colored eyes she said in a near whisper, "It's not a gift, but a curse. A curse I wish I didn't have."

Within a few months, the beautiful Hickory Ridge, Virginia, girl was deaf to all sounds. She heard nothing, either from her surroundings or from within herself as events happened somewhere else. She did not complain, but welcomed the quiet.

LATE IN THE EVENING

IT WAS THAT TIME, THAT LATE TIME IN the evening when the setting sun burns the western hills, when it is bright day then so suddenly night. I have walked that fleeting time so often, knowing I must hurry home. But either home is too far or there is something else I must see, and the dark catches me.

One evening when day would be only minutes longer and I knew it, I found myself far from home on the other side of Scarecorn Creek, on those old logging roads that cross the country where roads should never have come. They are not like other roads that someone surveyed and planned. No, these roads were made because the trees were cut and the trucks needed to go in. So they are red clay and rutted and gullied, and rain washes out big rocks that would stop any ordinary truck. But none of this will stop a logging truck. Or perhaps it is the men they will not stop.

I stood at the top of a high hill, looking down, and the level of the earth burned behind me. I wanted to go to the bottom of that road, but something barred my way. It was a man and a dog, and they seemed to come from a hole in the bottom of that hill as I watched and waited. Some

36

instinct, primitive and therefore long forgotten, pushed at my brain and I was afraid.

It was not the proportions of the man or dog that frightened me. No, they were quite ordinary in that respect. Nor was it their suddenness. In life, as I understand it, things happen suddenly. I think it was the time of day, a time of day when walkers should be home watching television and having supper. I was not at home. I was alone on a hill just before dark in a place where wild animals hold the night.

With that instinct of fear, I turned to my left and let the woods have me, though I did not go quickly, for there is unheeded danger in this. I took no time to admire the soft coldness about me or the last light blazing through the fading leaves. I just went like a soldier with a purpose, and my purpose was to be home before too much longer, where I would feel safe.

I suppose I was so focused on this purpose that I fell over the stone before my mind recognized that it was there. Yet there it was and there I lay, among the trees, among the hills, among the last of the light. Even now the night was stitching stars onto the sheltering quilt of the sky, and the sun burned like the rim of an eclipse on the western hills. I lay among the spent leaves, and when I raised my head I saw the familiar, but unexpected off-center shape of a gravestone. Turning only slightly, I saw still others.

I stood up quickly and looked about in horror, ringed as I was by stones marking death. Even as I stood there, an image walked before my mind—a man and a dog, the man dressed in black and the dog black by nature. I did not pause to look at names, my only want was to get away from it all. So I jumped the stone in my path and ran for home, unmindful of the hazards in that way of doing things.

I think back to many stories, but this one comes to

mind and I wonder, what was that man and dog? Did I cheat some fate written down in stone long ago? If I had lingered, would I be here now? And one last thing. Why in the smallness of my domain have I never found those gravestones again?

THE DUEL

TWELVE-YEAR-OLD BONNIE AND HER friend, thirteen-year-old Mary, came tearing into the Collinses' kitchen crying, "We seen a ghost!"

Bonnie's mother, Sara Collins, hugged the little girls and said, "It's all right, darlings. Tell me what you saw."

Hearing the commotion, Joe Collins, Bonnie's dad, joined the group in the kitchen. He asked, "What happened?"

"Well," said Bonnie, "we was up on the top of Henderson Hill. We was playing, when—" then Bonnie started to sob.

Mary cut in. "It was a lady, a beautiful lady. She walked across the meadow, she was barefooted, she was crying, and then she yelled something—"

Wiping her tears, Bonnie said, "Mommy, Daddy, that beautiful lady just walked up to us and disappeared."

"Yes," said Mary, "she just faded away. She's a ghost, a beautiful ghost, but a ghost."

Joe Collins took Mary to her parents' farmhouse. When he returned home, Sara and Bonnie, clad in night clothes, sat sipping cocoa and eating cookies.

Joe sat down and with a worried look said, "What do you think, Sara? Should we tell her that old ghost story?"

Sara Collins looked at her only child and said, "Yes, Joe, I think Bonnie's old enough."

Joe began to tell the tale of the ghost of Henderson Hill. Many years ago, in the hollow in back where the Collins place now stands, lived the Simmons family. They were better off than their neighbors in the rest of eastern Pickens County.

From birth young Josh was different from the other youngsters. He learned to read before he went to school, and all through grammar school he was a top student. Josh was a lonely child, and he didn't get along too well with the other country children.

When Josh was in sixth grade, a new boy joined the class. His name was Edward Strafford, and he was an orphan who lived with his kin in the next hollow.

When the boys graduated from eighth grade, the family decided that Josh would go to prep school in Cobb County. After much pleading by Josh, the Simmons family said they would pay for their son's best friend Edward to attend the same school. Edward wasn't the student Josh was, but in some ways he was smarter. He had decided that an education was better than farming.

The first day of school, Josh met a girl. Her name was Amy, and she lived over the hill from Josh in western Dawson County. It was love at first sight. A stunning girl, by graduation Amy had become a beautiful young lady.

All through prep school the three mountain kids went everywhere together. It was well known that Josh and Amy would marry right after graduation. On the night of their graduation, however, Edward declared his love for Amy. Stunned, Josh struck his friend. Maybe it was the shine the boys had drunk, but they decided to fight a duel on top of Henderson Hill at midnight.

Young kinfolk crowded the pasture as midnight approached. Shine was drunk in large quantities. Dozens of lanterns lit the pasture. Josh and Edward stood back to back, their pistols raised. They were to turn and fire at the count of seven.

Five, six, at the count of seven, a cloud blocked out the moon. Both boys turned, aimed their pistols—and a figure jumped between them screaming, "I love him." But it was too late. Two shots rang out, and Amy Collins fell mortally wounded.

"Mama," asked Bonnie, "what happened to the two boys?"

"Well, dear," said Sara Collins, "the boys were taken to the county jail. The next morning Josh was found hanged in his cell. Edward was released from jail and left the county for good."

"Did you ever see the ghost, Mama?" asked Bonnie.

"No, child, but your daddy did, and your uncle Lewis saw her a couple of times."

Bonnie, a thoughtful look on her young face, asked, "Why does the ghost lady come back?"

"Amy comes to the top of Henderson Hill every year on the anniversary of her death," answered Sara.

"Mama," asked Bonnie, "The ghost has the same last name as us?"

"Yes, dear," said Sara Collins. "You see, Amy Collins was your father's aunt."

CHURCHES

CHURCHES ARE IMPORTANT PLACES. THEY see almost every significant event in a person's life: christenings, baptisms, weddings, funerals. It makes one wonder if churches don't retain just a little of the emotions expressed within their sacred walls.

In a small community just east of Jasper is a pretty little white church with a rock foundation and an impressive spire that reaches to the sky. As is the custom around here, a narrow gravel road encircles this church and the old graveyard.

On moonless nights the brave, daring, or just plain foolish drive up to the church, park their cars, and get out. In the oppressive darkness, without aid of a flashlight, a short walk begins a unique adventure.

Three times around the church and graveyard one must walk, and if not alone, hands should be held. If alone, consider this a very brave thing to do.

When the thrice-around journey has been completed, approach the church from the east window nearest the front door. If one's courage has lasted this far, look through the clear glass and find a spectral wedding in progress.

A pale bride, a uniformed groom, their attendants,

and a minister in a dark frock coat stand at the front of the church, but no one fills the pews. Remain quiet. Even a small sound will frighten this vision away. If quiet, one will hear music but not voices in song, laughter but not conversation.

As with everything, the spectral wedding soon fades away into the mists of time. Now take out a flashlight or turn on the highbeams of the car. There is more to see.

There, at the east window and a little to the south, is a single grave with a small pink marble stone. The stone reads:

MISS JULIA RENAULT
Born June 22, 1898
Died June 24, 1917

Now, look to Miss Julia's right. You will find a simple government-issue stone and it reads:

CORPORAL JOHN SYMMONDS
Born December 11, 1895
Died 1917
At the battle of Chateau-Thierry
Buried at Flanders Fields, France

The spectral wedding inside the church is a wedding that never took place, as Miss Julia's fiancé never came home from France, at least not alive.

* * *

Serious ghost hunting is not for the faint of heart. Nor is it wise to hunt alone. Hunting is best done in pairs or groups so the participants can compare notes afterward. The account of someone alone can easily be marked down to simple fear rather than spectral activity. So when one goes to that double-doored Baptist church in the fork of the road west of Jasper, the county seat of Pickens County, it should not be alone.

Go at night, and when the car pulls into the black gravel parking lot, extinguish all lights and cut the engine. But don't get out of the car. It is safer if everyone simply sits right there in the close darkness and listens to the nocturnal sounds all around.

While waiting, whispered jokes won't hurt, but they won't change what is to be seen, either. Be patient, and it will happen. It always does.

Someone in the car will say, "What's that?" and all hearts will catch and all eyes will strain to see.

"It looks like a light," someone else will say.

Then it is seen. All of them are seen. Little lights, dancing among the gravestones like fireflies, only much larger. Swamp gases? There is no swamp nearby. Car headlights reflected on the shiny stones? The dancing lights are not on the stones. They're around them.

If someone gets out of the car and tries to follow the lights or find their sources, the lights will vanish, like frightened deer, out of sight. So stay in the car and watch until they choose to leave, until their play is over. They will fade away in time.

*　　*　　*

If you have made it this far on our tour of churches, I admire you greatly. I hope we have saved the best for last.

The Primitive Baptist church in question does not meet every week for Sunday services. There is no Sunday school, no vacation Bible school. For months at a time, especially in the winter, nothing happens in the little weathered church in the westernmost reaches of Pickens County. Only an occasional funeral, the traditional homecoming Sunday, perhaps a week-long revival, and a few services a year fill the rough pews with people. The rest of the year the church is closed, and whatever occupies it is certainly not human.

The church is in an area known as Long Creek, and it is easy to get lost there. The houses are few and far between, and sometimes the people are not happy to see you. You must scout out the church during the day, because it is easy to miss.

This church has no bell tower or vestibule, indoor plumbing or electricity. In the small graveyard, the wildflowers abound in summer. There are several handmade stones, some with the word *dide* rather than *died*, and it is profound to read the heartfelt inscriptions, to trace the words and primitive scribing, to realize the memory of these people would be lost if not for those stones.

To the side of the graveyard is a well with a windlass but no bucket or rope, and a piece of slate covers the hole. When there are services of any kind, someone brings a rope and a bucket and the devout get their water from the icy depths. It is good, no doubt, on a hot summer evening during revival to go out and have a long drink from that well.

The only other structure on the sacred grounds is a long table with a shelter over it. This is used for homecoming when folks spread their dinner and eat the fine cooking of members and visitors among the carefully groomed and flower-bedecked graves of their ancestors.

Find your way to this church in the daylight and remember the way; and be patient, for distances in the country are deceptive at night. When you have found your way back in the dark, get out of your car and walk up the church steps. The whitewashed double front doors of the unpainted wooden structure are never locked.

If you wish, you may light your way with a flashlight or a candle, but be careful of fire. The church is very old, the wood dry, and it sits on the foundation of an even older church that burned long before your oldest living relative was born.

Once inside the church, find the rough plank pew at the very back and on the left. Walk down to the end of it until you are against the splintery wooden wall. Now you must sit and extinguish your light. If you are lucky there will be some shaving of a moon shining through the tall windows, casting long shadows on everything around you.

If the moon is your ally, you will see something of the interior of the church. You will notice there is no piano, no pulpit, no hymnals, no fonts or pictures or adornment of any kind. There is a slightly raised place at the front for the preachers to walk when the spirit takes hold of them. It reminds you that this church is a house of God where the Word is spoken and any foolishness is out of place.

You close your eyes and can hear the voices raised in song, and perhaps you think how strange they sound without music to accompany them. Almost like a primitive chant brought forth from long ago. Suddenly your heart is hammering against your breast.

What is it? you wonder. Your eyes fly open and you stare straight ahead, your vision taking a moment to focus. When you finally can see, you see only what you observed previously, but then you feel something. Something cold. Something behind you. You turn and encounter only a blank wooden wall. Once again you look forward at the moonlight streaming through the windows. And you feel it again. Only this time it feels more persistent.

Someone—or is it something?—has touched you on the shoulder. You recognize the impression of . . . is it fingers? . . . cold fingers, like ice grasping your shoulder until it goes numb. You do not turn around again. You desperately want out of that place.

From your dark corner you bolt, your feet pounding across the pine floor to the double front doors. You fling them open and stumble down the plank steps. You run to your car. You don't remember parking so far away.

Once in the safety of your car, you quickly lock the doors and cannot keep your eyes from straying up as you start the engine and put the car into gear. You wonder if you see something standing at the doors you have left open, but you reason it could be a trick of the moonlight.

Fleetingly, you feel foolish, stupid for being frightened, for going to this place, for imagining yourself touched by an icy hand; but then your subconscious reminds you and you cannot wait to leave.

Perhaps your heart stops its furious beating after you cross the bridge over Scarecorn Creek that marks the invisible border of Long Creek. All you know is you are not going back to that little Primitive Baptist church for a while, and never again when the sun has fallen in the west. Not even when the moon is your ally.

THE CRYING MIST

SEVENTEEN-YEAR-OLD VICKY COLLINS AND Tommy Warren, her nineteen-year-old boyfriend, had been to the movie theater in the nearby town of Benton. It was just another Saturday night here in rural southern Appalachia, and it was the last night to see *Star Wars*. The twosome had caught the first show and it was still early, around 9:30. Vicky didn't have to be home till 11:00. Besides, she was staying over with her grandmother this night, and the old woman was always bending the rules for her granddaughter.

Just after crossing the county line, Tommy turned onto a dirt road leading to Clayton Lake. The sky was bright with a full moon. Tommy stopped the car at the road's end. They could see the water shimmering with moonlight. Tommy pulled Vicky into his arms. He kissed her gently, and she responded. The night was warm, and all the car windows were rolled down.

After only a few minutes, a light wind rose and Vicky heard crying. She pushed herself away from Tommy.

"What's wrong?" the boy asked.

"Listen," Vicky said. "I hear somebody crying."

Tommy listened. He didn't hear anything but lake

noises like frogs, crickets, and occasionally a jumping fish.

"It's just katydids," he said, reaching to draw the girl to him once more.

Vicky still heard the pitiful sobbings. She couldn't determine where they were coming from, but she knew they were not alone here by the lake as Tommy thought.

"Maybe we should leave," she said to the young man seated beside her.

"It's early. We don't have to go yet," came the reply.

Vicky shivered as a chill ran through her. Her heart quickened its pace and a strange, ugly fear wrapped around her.

"Something's not right," she whispered. "I do hear somebody crying. A woman."

Before she could continue, an icy-cold, vaporlike mist wisped in the car's window and hung like tendriled fingers before her. Vicky was paralyzed with fear. Even though she was screaming inside, only small, whimpering sounds escaped her lips.

The mist appeared to take on life, and it drifted quickly from the car and floated across the ground to an old willow tree standing near the water's edge.

The long, spindly branches stirred slightly as if they too were crying, and Vicky heard the sounds again. It was a soulful sound of agony and unspeakable pain. The mist took on shape and form to stand beneath the tree's darkness.

"Take me home," Vicky managed to say in a strange tone. "Now. Tommy, get me out of here. This is an evil place."

The boy reached to touch the girl. She was pale as death and just as cold. He hadn't seen or heard anything evil, but he did see the terror in Vicky's face.

Tommy cranked the car, and soon they were back on the main road. Vicky began to tremble, and tears flowed uncontrollably from her eyes. Tommy was scared. He didn't know what was wrong, but something unnatural had happened to Vicky. She was so cold, so pale against the warm summer night.

"What happened back there?" he asked, slowing the car.

"Don't stop," she said. "Please don't stop. Get me far away from this place. Something terribly bad happened there."

Vicky became silent. Tommy held her close to him with one arm as he accelerated and hurried to get the girl to her grandmother's house. Once there, he nearly had to carry her inside, she was trembling so.

"What's happened here?" Grandma Collins asked. "What have you done to this child?"

"I didn't do anything. I swear," the boy answered. "I don't know what's wrong. We were at Clayton Lake, and she kept hearing something."

"Grandma," the girl sobbed. "I did hear something."

"Come on. Let's get you to bed. You'll feel better in the morning. Go on home, Tommy. Vicky will call you tomorrow," Grandma Collins said, leading the girl to a bedroom.

Soon Vicky was in bed under heavy covers, and still she shivered with a bone-chilling cold. Tears still slid from her eyes, and she couldn't shake the fear of what she had seen and heard.

Grandma brought a cup of hot herbal tea and sat down beside her granddaughter.

The girl sat up and shakily took the hot brew. "Grandma," the girl said. "Tell me about Clayton Lake. Has anything bad ever happened there?"

"Well, old folks say the place is haunted," Grandma said. "But that's just talk."

"Tell me," Vicky said, sipping the tea. "What do they say?"

"Maybe tomorrow. You need to sleep now. You're just too tired. I told your mama working and going to school was too much for you," the woman said, patting the girl's arm.

"No, Grandma. Tell me now. I need to know. Please," Vicky pleaded.

"Well," the woman began, "the tale was, a long time ago, a young girl, I think she was a Tatum, and a boy from Benton was going to run off and get married. They was just kids, about fourteen or fifteen years old, and her pa found out and shot the boy."

"Did it happen at Clayton Lake?" Vicky asked, beginning to warm up some.

"Well, I was told it all happened out there," the woman said.

"What else?" Vicky asked. "What happened to the girl?"

"Don't know," Grandma Collins answered. "I've heard folks say that sometimes a girl can be heard crying out there by the lake, somewhere close to the county line. But that's just old haunt tales. I heard all that stuff when I was just a girl. It was just to scare us younguns and keep us away from there."

"I heard her, Grandma," the girl said, staring into the teacup. "And I didn't just hear her pitiful cries. I saw her there at the willow by the water's edge. She's still in pain after all this time. She's still crying."

Vicky Collins says she has never gone back to Clayton Lake. She's now a grown woman, and to this very day she gets an icy chill whenever she passes the old lake road. She won't talk about what happened all those years ago, but she says that evil hangs heavy in the air there about the county line. A few can feel the haunted cold on that stretch of road, but no one else has ever mentioned seeing floating mist.

PREDAWN TRAVELERS

LOIS AND ELLA KEENAN, SISTERS-IN-LAW, were staying overnight at Ella's house on the little family farm outside Murphy, North Carolina. Their husbands were gone off on a hunting trip somewhere in the Couhutta Mountains.

The men would return before very late the next day as it was only about a forty-mile drive. But camping out the night before deer season opened was sort of tradition for the men, and it also gave the two women a chance to visit without male interruption.

The early part of the night passed quickly with the women sharing local gossip and exchanging new recipes and talking about the upcoming holidays. November was always a busy planning time for country folk.

Morning dawned bitter cold. Lois had to go home early to tend her farm animals. It was around 5:00 A.M. when she got into her car to make the ten-mile drive home. Daylight had yet to make any kind of break in the eastern sky, and stars still twinkled brightly overhead.

Lois had traveled two or three miles when she saw someone carrying a lantern walking toward her. The person was in the center of the road, and Lois's presence, even with the big automobile moving ever closer, didn't phase the walking person. Lois believed the person would surely move to one side or the other as she honked the horn. She slowed but was afraid to stop as there were no houses close by on the isolated country road.

The woman was very scared—afraid to stop, afraid to try to get past the person carrying the lantern, afraid she might run over whoever it was that nearly blocked her path. Lois became almost terrorized as she moved steadily onward. Yet as the two early morning travelers closed the space between them, the person with the lantern disappeared, was gone, or maybe was merely transplaced in time.

Lois later learned that early in the 1900s, a man had been found murdered here on this isolated country road. It had happened long ago on a cold November morning. The man had been shot twice and lay crumpled on the very same road she had traveled. A few feet from where the man lay, a broken lantern was found. It had probably been carried by the man who had walked the road in the early predawn hours of that bitter cold winter morning.

A Brief Encounter

In SOUTHERN APPALACHIA SUMMER LIN-
gers well into October, but nights begin to grow cool
sometime in September. The day can start out with frost
on the ground, and by noon it is eighty degrees or better.
The real beauty, weather-wise, is the bell-like clarity of
the blue skies.

On a late October day when the sun shone with that
odd quality peculiar to a clear autumn day, Amanda drove
to work at two in the afternoon. For eight hours she stood
behind the cash register of a convenience store. To those
frequenting such places, this sort of labor looks easy, even
undemanding, but standing for eight hours, handling
thousands of dollars in transactions, and closing a store for
the night can be stressful to the mind and body.

Amanda had been working at the store just over a
month and had finally become comfortable with the job.
The difficult part was closing at night. At eleven o'clock
she was always happy to see one of the sheriff's deputies
come in and wait with her while she counted down the
register and put the money in the safe. It was an intense
time as on some nights the thousands of dollars could go
into five digits. At least, Amanda often thought, she did

not have to make a night deposit at one of the four local banks.

On one particular night everything went smoothly at work. Amanda put in her eight hours, the deputy was there, and she gave him the last of the coffee while she counted down the register. When all was complete, she locked up, waved to the deputy, got in her car, and drove the eleven miles home.

It was well after one o'clock when she went to bed. Even when she was not working a late shift she was always late to bed, so on this night she was not overly tired.

"I came in from work," Amanda said, "had something to eat, watched some television, and then went to bed."

She had done this every night since starting work at the store, but this was not like every other night. There was a full moon, and the yard of Amanda's rural home was bathed in a silver glow.

"We had started turning the air conditioner off at night," she said. "And we were opening our windows. One window in my room faces the driveway, and the other faces the creek."

To the west of the house is a valley, and as a border of that valley Scarecorn Creek winds its way west, then north, until it tumbles into Talking Rock Creek. She could hear Scarecorn Creek through her open window.

"At that time my bed was positioned right against the window facing the creek," Amanda continued. "The ledge was low enough so I could put part of my pillow on it. I liked the fresh air."

As usual, when the woman went to bed she did not go right to sleep. Some people fall asleep once their heads touch the pillow. Others must spend time thinking about their day.

"I eventually fell asleep," she explained. "I think

about everything I've done all day until I'm suddenly asleep. Anyway, I do know I had gone to sleep, but suddenly I was wide awake and looking out my window into the yard."

From her bed so near the window Amanda had a clear view of the back yard, bordered by trees and a thick growth of blackberries. A wooden deck takes up a great deal of it.

"I was lying there," the woman said, "and I was somehow wrapped up in my covers. I couldn't move my arms. Maybe that's part of what woke me up. Anyway, I was looking out the window, through the screen, and standing there in the yard, where the juniper bush has grown up, was a man."

The man was dressed in gray or light blue. He had on a slouch hat. Crossed over his chest were leather straps. On his left hip was a gun in a holster, and on his right was a canteen. His right hand was resting on the canteen.

"He stood about twelve feet away," Amanda reported, "but in the moonlight I could see how young he was. He was a Civil War soldier. I realized it right away."

The young soldier simply stood there. He did not move or speak. He seemed harmless, and the woman was not afraid of him.

"I wanted to raise my hand and tell him to go," Amanda said, "but my arms were pinned by the covers. Finally I told him to go away, and he faded into nothing. I eventually went back to sleep."

In Georgia there were many battles and minor engagements. There were also many soldiers. Some of the last stands of the Confederacy took place only a few miles from Scarecorn Creek. It is not difficult to believe a young soldier may still be about.

"For a long time," the woman said, "I didn't like that spot. Even in the daytime. Actually, I think there's something strange about the whole area. Three Valentine's

Days in a row I've found heart-shaped stones in my path when I was out walking."

Amanda shrugs, and then she smiles. Was it a dream? Or was the spirit of a long-dead Rebel soldier standing in the moonlight? One supposes it could depend on a certain way of thinking. Of course, the notion of a Rebel soldier as a ghost still parading about in his finery is particularly romantic, and one would prefer to think pride of place and time is not lost in death but lingers on into our time for a privileged living few to witness.

CEMETERY RIDER

NATHAN ROLLINS RECALLS AS A YOUNG man how churches marked outreaches of the counties as settlements. Farmhouses were sparsely sprinkled throughout the Georgia, Tennessee, and North Carolina mountains, and roads were mere wagon ruts. Walking was about the only way of getting to your destination.

One day, Nathan was making his way past the Big Creek Church House when a soft summer rain began to fall onto the dusty, red-clay road. Nathan hurried his pace, and upon nearing a bridge, a rider on a big red horse raced through the creek toward him. The rider, wearing a dusty black suit and drooping black hat, looked at the young man walking on the road. A strange look glazed the rider's eyes as he sat tall in the saddle and turned, looking over his shoulder to stare at Nathan as the horse raced by.

The young man said when the horse had passed, as if knowing where to go, it turned sharply to the left and made its way up a steep bank with little or no effort at all. Both the big red horse and the tall rider dressed in black disappeared amid the gravestones of the church cemetery.

The young man said neither horse nor rider made any sound as they splashed through the water stampeding past him to the nearby resting place of the dead.

Cemetery Rider

Nathan looked but said he saw no prints left by the huge beast in the soft earth moistened by the summer rain.

Nathan often wondered if perhaps it was a ghost horse, returning a lost spirit to its rightful resting place.

ZION HILL HAUNTINGS

"YOU SHOULD HAVE TALKED TO GRANNY before she died if you was interested in ghost stories. She was just full of them. And she just loved to tell them, too," Martha Sanford said, shaking her head sadly as if she wished she could hear more of Granny's stories about ghosts and hauntings and mysteries.

"The tales she used to tell," Martha laughed. "You know, she lived up on Zion Hill in the Mountain Town community. Always was weird goings-on up there. I think they probably still are."

Martha began to recall stories the old woman told before her death only a few years earlier.

Years ago it was common for the people of this rural area to take folks in for the night who were just passing through. One time there was a young man traveling through the Zion Hill area of the county when night fell. He stopped at the first house he came to. A man, Granny thought his name was Gomer Parker, and his three children lived there. The wife and mother of the children had recently died. The young man asked if he could stay overnight at their home. The man of the house said he could sleep in the front room, but not near the doorway.

The young man asked, "Why?"

"You'll see," came the answer.

The night grew long, and soon the children and the man went to the two bedrooms to sleep, the children in one, the man in the other. The traveler made a pallet on the floor in front of the fireplace with quilts given to him by the man. He lay down and was soon asleep. Later, in the deepest, darkest part of the night, the young traveler was awakened as the front door opened and a round, ball-like light floated through the doorway. It continued its journey into the children's room, hovering over each child. Then, it came out of the children's room and went into the man's room. After a few moments, the ball-like light left the house through the still-open front door. As it retreated, the door slowly closed, leaving the house dark in the night and its occupants knowing someone or some-thing watched over them as they slept.

* * *

Granny said there were witches along with the ghosts on Zion Hill, too. Said they had awfully strong powers. Nobody crossed one particular witch living up there. Well, not after word of just how strong she really was spread about the settlement.

Seems this witch woman got mad at a neighbor over something and said she'd get even. Said the neighbor would be sorry for crossing her.

After thinking or conjuring or doing whatever witch women do when crossed, the witch woman took a dish-rag down to her neighbor's barn and milked the cow with the dishrag till the poor cow was dry. The cow never gave another drop of milk.

* * *

Two of the Akins brothers, Sam, the older of the two, and Clem, and a friend of Sam's, Robert Sacket, were somewhere on Mountain Town Creek. It was late fall and cold weather was beginning in the mountains. The men had been drinking pretty heavily, and Sam and Robert were acting up pretty bad. They poked fun and pulled silly pranks on the younger boy until he had had enough. Saying that he was too cold, Clem found an excuse to leave and go home.

Clem climbed on his old mule and headed the animal in the direction of home. He was a bit drunk, and he was mad at his brother for playing his foolishness on him.

It was more than a mile to the house, and as the mule came to a deep hollow in the road, it balked. Clem kicked the animal, urging him onward. Still the mule refused to go forward.

Clem looked around, thinking maybe a snake or opossum or some other nighttime animal was spooking the stubborn beast. There was nothing there. It was then Clem looked upon the high bank overhanging the road. There Clem saw a hooded something crouched near the edge.

"I've had enough, Sam," Clem said, thinking it was another of his brother's tricks. "Leave me alone. I'm going home."

The mule stomped the ground. Clem thought he would fire his gun and scare Sam. Just as the young man backed the hammers of the shotgun, the hooded thing stood and threw back the hood.

Clem said he let the mule go any which way it wanted to go then. Said he had never been that scared in all his life at what he saw underneath that hood, and to this day no one knows what he saw. Clem either couldn't, or wouldn't, tell.

*   *   *

There always were quilting bees, or as Granny called them, "quilting parties," during the winter months in the Mountain Town community. The women would gather at one of their houses and, with everyone stitching around the frames hanging from the ceiling, in a day's time a quilt could be stitched from beginning to end.

Everybody always brought food, and in the middle of the afternoon the women would stop quilting and would spread a table with the food they had brought from home. It was good fellowship for the women as they hardly ever got out except for church, and somebody always had a new quilt at the end of the day.

The Zion Hill women of the Mountain Town community would sometimes complete as many as twenty quilts in a winter. Of course, there were about ten women, but they were known for their good work—short, neat stitches—and when finished, the quilt was a thing of beauty and gave warmth on bitter cold winter nights.

Granny said that at one quilting the subject of witches was brought up, and one young woman, Mary Rose Harmon, really took interest.

"You know," she said, "I always wished I was a witch."

"Surely not," someone replied. "Maybe a queen, but not a witch."

"Yes, a witch," Mary Rose said, re-threading her needle with heavy cotton quilting thread.

When the women stopped to eat, an elderly woman, Tilly Ravenwood, made her way to where Mary Rose sat behind the long, oilcloth-covered table.

"Do you really want to be a witch?" Tilly asked in a low tone.

"Yes," the younger woman answered. "I've always wanted to be one."

"Are you sure?" the old woman asked, staring at Mary Rose as if trying to read her thoughts.

"I wouldn't say it if I didn't mean it," Mary Rose said, wondering why this old woman kept questioning her so.

"Okay, if you're sure," the old woman said. "I think I can help you."

"How?" the young woman asked, now eager to know more.

Tilly told Mary Rose to go to the old Bradberry house the following Saturday night before midnight if she was serious about becoming a witch. Mary Rose had passed the old house many times. It looked kind of spooky, sitting back in a thicket of pine trees. Nobody lived there, and the house was nearly falling down.

When the time came, Mary Rose approached the house. It was all lit up, and upon entering she saw a fire in the fireplace and maybe a dozen people milling about in the large front room.

Tilly Ravenwood approached the girl, a smile on her wrinkled face. She directed the girl to a rug in front of the fireplace.

"If you're sure about this," Tilly said, "all you have to do is lay down here on this bearskin rug, put one hand on the top of your head and the other on the bottom of your feet, and say all that lays between my hands belongs to the Devil, and a witch you'll become."

Mary Rose lay down on the rug, placing one hand atop her head, the other on the bottom of her feet. She became frightened, and as the group gathered around encouraging her to repeat, "All that lays between my hands belongs to the Devil," she wished she were home.

"Say it," Tilly Ravenwood said, her tone stern.

"All that lays between my hands," the girl began in a shaky voice, then drawing a deep breath continued, "belongs to the Lord."

Instantly, the fire and lights were out and gone, and the room was empty of people. Everything had vanished as if it had never been there at all, except for the young woman who remained alone in the cold, dark, falling-down house.

THE HUDSON PLACE

IN THE 1890s WHEN JOHN HUDSON DE-
cided to build his summer home, he didn't build in the
mountain resort area. The Atlanta railroad magnate built
his retreat in the western section of Culver County, a farming area. Hudson's estate wasn't a mansion in the usual
sense—he had built a farm-style house with some excep-
tions. A veranda was built around the entire building,
and French doors led off the veranda into the house itself.

Hudson had bought an abandoned farm off Church
Road, which was the main road serving the farms in western Culver County. The Hudson place did not have exten-
sive gardens or bright green lawns; the woods grew
almost to the house. Young lads living on the farms in
back of Hudson's would cut across the fields and walk
around the house via the veranda. Thus they saved themselves a mile-and-a-half walk to school, the creek, or the
general store.

According to a local legend, in 1912 an event occurred that left the Hudson place haunted.

John Hudson was known in Atlanta as a rake. Despite
his age, he had many intimate parties at his summer
home. On that fatal day, John and a young actress—nobody ever knew her name—were driving on Church Road

in Hudson's carriage. For some reason when they passed over a small bridge across Cherokee Creek, the carriage crashed through the guardrail and dumped both occupants into the creek.

Marvin Darcy and his two sons were walking along Church Road when the carriage went in the creek. They jumped in and pulled out both people. John Hudson was all right, but the girl was unconscious. Marvin Darcy swore the girl was alive when they carried her to the Hudson place. Ben Harper also said later that he heard screams coming from the Hudson place that night. The girl, however, was pronounced dead, and that started stories of the old place being haunted. To this day many people report hearing screams coming from the Hudson place even though no one was there.

"Grandpa, will you tell us a story?" asked nine-year-old Louann.

"Yes, Grandpa, tell us a ghost story," cried ten-year-old Butch.

It was a typical summer day in southern Appalachia. It had been hot and muggy, and now late afternoon thunder and lightning crashed around our grandparents' farmhouse. The oil lamps were lit on the dining room table. We had just finished cookies and lemonade.

"Please, Grandpa," said seven-year-old Sarah. "Tell us a ghost story."

Grandpa lit his pipe and started his story. The boy was about Jim's age—twelve—and his mama sent him over to the general store. He cut through the Hudson place, walked around the veranda, and on to Church Road. He went to the store and was on his way back home.

As he walked along, a big Packard convertible roared past him. The sporty car went about a hundred yards, then stopped. There were two people in the car. One was Jerry

Hudson, grandson of old John Hudson. He was driving, but it was the young lady with Jerry who drew the boy's attention. He had never seen anyone like her. Oh, maybe at the picture show. She sure is beautiful, he thought.

The young girl yelled, "Come on little boy, we'll give you a ride."

The boy got in the car and was intoxicated by the smell of the lady's perfume. She wore a dress that barely covered her, and her eyes were bright as she hugged the boy.

Jerry Hudson was a dark, cruel-looking young man, and he was known in the county as a young sport.

The girl asked, "What's your name, little boy?" He told her and noticed another aroma. Moonshine!

It happened on the little bridge over Cherokee Creek. Jerry Hudson was going too fast, and they crashed through the guardrail and plunged into the creek. The boy easily swam to the surface. He saw Jerry Hudson climbing out of the creek.

The girl surfaced, coughing and screaming. The boy grabbed her hair and pulled her to shore. Two cars had parked on opposite sides of the bridge. The occupants pulled the boy and the girl to safety. The girl was hysterical, but otherwise seemed all right. A man offered to take Jerry and the girl to the Hudson place, and they agreed.

The boy left, taking the shortcut through the Hudson place. He arrived home and to his dismay found nobody there. He reasoned that his folks must have gone to the creek when they heard about the accident. News traveled fast, even in those days.

It was dusk when the boy headed back to the creek. He cut across the fields and walked onto the Hudson place veranda. He was just passing an open French door when he heard a scream. He turned and looked into the room.

The next thing he knew someone was shouting at him.

"Hey, boy, get in this truck. Your folks are worried sick about you. They heard you was drowned." This was said by the boy's uncle Luke. He hadn't even heard the truck come up to him.

The boy got in the truck and looked around. He was miles from home, and it was daybreak. He had no idea how he had gotten here. When he arrived home, his folks laughed and cried. They thought he had drowned. Mama saw he was leery, almost scared.

She asked, "What happened? Why are you looking so spooked?"

The boy said he didn't know; he had seen something but he didn't know what. Mama then called the local doctor.

Doc Edwards said, "The boy has a mental block on what he thinks he saw. He'll be all right in a day or two."

No matter how hard he tried, the boy couldn't remember anything after he looked through the French doors.

The next day Jerry Hudson left the old place. When questioned by the sheriff, he said that the girl had left the night before. He didn't know her name—he met her at a watering hole in Atlanta.

Jerry Hudson and the girl were never seen again in Culver County. The old Hudson place went to ruin, but many nights folks around here hear screams seemingly coming from two women.

"Oh, Grandpa," Sarah cried, "How do we know that old story's true?"

"Why, darling, it's true enough," Grandpa answered as he lit his pipe. "You see, I was that little boy."

THE DISAPPEARING WAGON

CLYDE AND MABLE AARON LIVED IN THE Big Creek section of Gilmer County years ago, long before there were any blacktopped asphalt highways in the area. The roads were hard-packed red clay with splatterings of crushed gravel in the rough, pothole spots.

Occasionally, Mable's sister Pauline would come to visit the couple for a few days. She lived some fifteen miles away on the other side of the county. The sisters were close, and these visits served to strengthen their family bonds and to keep them up with the goings-on in two different locations of the county.

Clyde had a car, and on one such planned visit he agreed to go and get Pauline. Pauline had her bags packed and was ready when Clyde arrived. As they made their journey across the country roads, Pauline and Clyde talked about the Aaron children and how fast they all were growing up.

As Clyde approached the road fronting Macedonia Church, he saw up ahead of them a covered wagon pulled by a decrepit-looking old mule. Because there were no turnoff roads for a couple of miles and the road was wider here, he tried to pass the creeping wagon by the old country church.

Try as he might, Clyde couldn't get close enough to the wagon to overtake it. Rounding a curve in the road just beyond the church house, he saw that the wagon was gone. There was no trace of it. As the car traveled through the Big Creek area, there was not a track of wagon or mule anywhere on the narrow dirt road.

Both Clyde and Pauline were shocked when the wagon disappeared from in front of them. When they arrived at the Aaron home, Pauline trembled and her voice shook as she told Mable the strange tale.

"It was there, and then it just disappeared. Like it had floated away or something," Pauline said, trying to explain the mystery to herself.

"Maybe it did," Mable said. "Maybe it was lost and, finding the old church, realized it was finally home."

There has never been a report of anyone else seeing the mysterious, disappearing mule and wagon but Clyde Aaron and his sister-in-law, Pauline.

THE GOAT HOUSE

MARK AND MAGGIE CLAMBERED UP THE stairs, careful to stay close to the wall. The stairs no longer had a rail, and if you lost your footing you might plunge to the floor far below. Actually, the floor was not that far from the top of the stairs, but it seemed that way to the two imaginative teenagers.

At the top of the stairs was a door. Lately it had been sticking because the house was coming off its old rock foundations. After every storm with even a little wind, the house leaned a little more. The cousins knew that one day they would not be able to go into the abandoned house at all for fear of it falling on their heads.

It had never been an impressive house—just three rooms. But the cousins lived in modern, ranch-style houses, and anything with stairs was a novelty. So in their fertile minds the house had taken on the proportions of a mansion and was just as full of mystery as any mansion had ever been.

Once on the second floor of their pretend mystery mansion, Mark and Maggie collapsed into a heap of backpacks filled with the spoils of a day's rambling and the remains of their lunch. The cousins had been out since ten that mid-autumn Saturday morning, and now, at four in the afternoon, they were tired but excited by their adventures.

"Anything to drink?" Mark asked as he rummaged through his pack and looked at Maggie's unopened pack with interest.

"Water," Maggie said and retrieved the half-filled bottle from her backpack.

"Nothing else?" he asked with hope.

"Crackers and peanut butter," Maggie answered with a shrug.

"I'll have some water," Mark decided, and while the cousins passed the plastic bottle back and forth a silence fell, broken only by the rain and an occasional angry rumble of thunder.

A breeze sprang up, blowing the cool rain into the room through the two narrow windows flanking the crumbling fireplace. Maggie and Mark sat near the windows, against a wall not yet affected by the shifting of the house. Their backs were against the beaded board wall as their eyes watched the rain battering the last of the leaves from the ancient oak in what had once been the front yard of the house.

Finally the silence was too much. "Is this house really haunted?" Mark asked, feeling an involuntary shiver go through his body while the skin on his arms got goose flesh.

"Granny says it is," Maggie replied.

"How would she know?"

"She lived here when she was a girl," Maggie answered and reached for a slightly stale peanut butter cracker to munch.

"What happened when she was living here?" Mark asked with avid interest.

"Well, it would happen at night," Maggie said just as thunder crackled nearby.

"What would happen at night?" Mark asked, his

voice low and his imagination working overtime in an effort for a really good scare.

"She'd be in bed with her sisters," Maggie explained. "In those days the girls all slept together. Anyway, Granny said she'd be just about asleep and something would jerk the covers clean off the bed."

"What was it?"

"I don't know. So they'd light the lamp and shine it all around, especially under the bed, but there wouldn't be anything to see. Then they'd tuck the covers back in around them and put out the lamp, only to have the covers jerked off again."

"Did they leave?"

"No. They couldn't go anywhere. They were farming, and they had a crop to bring in. Anyway, sometimes Granny would feel a cold, icy hand on her legs. Her sisters felt it, too. Sometimes they even saw something moving around under the covers at the foot of the bed, only there wouldn't be anything there when they'd look. A couple of times the bed was pushed around the room."

Mark's blue eyes were big as he said, "Sounds like a poltergeist to me."

"What's that?"

"You know, a noisy spirit. They're not like real ghosts that you can see and hear. They just move things around and throw things and pull the covers off of you."

"But they could hear it," Maggie informed him. "Granny said she'd be in the kitchen while everybody else was in the fields, and she'd hear somebody laugh behind her. She'd turn, and there wouldn't be anybody else in the room. They heard the laughing all over the house. Outside, too, in the yard."

"Did they ever see it?"

"Maybe. But just out of the corner of their eyes. Finally their mother came and spent the night with them in this very room," Maggie lowered her voice. "See, Granny's mother was tired of all the noise. She thought the girls were doing it themselves, just trying to scare their brothers. She didn't believe something was actually bothering them."

Mark grinned. "So what happened to her?"

"Well, she started to spend the night, but no sooner did she have the covers pulled up over her than they were jerked off onto the floor. That happened two or three times. Then when she got the covers tucked in really good, whatever it was started playing around under the covers at the foot of the bed. When she told it to stop, the bed started shaking and moving around the room. I imagine she got real mad and told it to stop it and get out of the house and go back to wherever it had come from. It just laughed at her. Granny said you didn't laugh at her mother. She'd take a stick of stove wood to your backside."

Mark laughed. "I bet she was ready to hit something."

"Granny said she had never seen her mother madder," Maggie confirmed. "Finally, her mother got out of bed and stood in the middle of the room and had a talk with whatever was haunting the house. She told it plain that it was not welcome in her house and it would get out or she would make it sorry. It laughed again, and she started quoting the Bible at it. That made the thing really mad, and it started moving the bed around like it was on wheels. Granny said she and her sisters were terrified, but her mother wasn't. She was too mad to be terrified."

"Did it leave?"

Maggie shook her head. "No. It spoke. It said, 'You can go, but I'll be staying since this is my home and not yours.' I guess Granny's mother had had enough, because they packed up in the night and went to a relative's to stay. They never stayed in the house again, though a few other people did."

"Did they stay long?"

"No. Finally nobody came here anymore, and it

started falling down. I don't suppose it's got too many years left."

Mark began to agree, but the words froze in his throat. He and Maggie stared at each other in fright as her mouth dropped open. They had heard the unmistakable sound of laughter downstairs, and now someone or something was crossing the floor and coming up the narrow stairs.

"What is it?" Mark desperately asked.

"I don't know," Maggie choked out. "Go look."

"You go look."

Maggie shook her head and hugged her backpack to her chest. Both cousins looked toward the stair and saw a face slowly rising. It was wide in the cheeks and had large brown eyes, a pointed beard, and two curving horns.

"Oh, no!" Maggie gasped and fell back against the wall.

"I don't believe it!" Mark yelled in shock, scaring the thing in the process and sending it back down the stairs in a frightened flight. "It was a goat!"

Maggie and Mark laughed loud and long to relieve the tension around them. Finally, they straightened up and looked at each other and smiled. Mark pretended to wipe sweat from his brow and Maggie laughed again.

"Don't you dare tell a soul," Mark warned.

"I'm just glad it wasn't a ghost," Maggie said. "And don't worry. Do you think I want people to know I was scared of a goat?"

The cousins chuckled as they repacked their things. Outside the storm was quickly passing, but one last gust of wind swept through the house and pushed the door to the stairs closed with a resounding slam. It was the last fright of the day for the duo.

*   *   *

The house is gone now. The old foundation finally fell away to nothing, and the house collapsed into itself. Once a small group of goats used the house for shelter.

They would go inside and up the stairs to one of the windows next to the crumbling chimney. From the window they would leap out onto the chimney ledge on the outside of the house and perhaps pretend to be mountain goats. The goats are gone now, too.

The cousins are long since grown up. He became an artist and now lives in Atlanta. She became a writer and still lives near where the old house once stood.

APPALACHIAN EXORCIST

IRIS ENTERED THE RAMBLING TWO-STORY farmhouse, built sometime around the turn of the century on the Georgia-Tennessee-North Carolina border. According to her long-time friends who had lived here less than a year, it was haunted.

The silence felt heavy about the living room as the woman slipped the pack from her shoulder to the wide-plank floor and seated herself on the overstuffed sofa. She was waiting for night to fall.

She was just a country woman, but she was receptive to unexplained phenomena, and after careful research, which included talking to a Catholic priest, she was going to exorcise the ghost in this house.

In the cool of the evening she recalled what her friends Mike and Barbara had told her.

Incidents began soon after they had moved here to the Appalachian foothills from Atlanta. They loved the old rustic house with its big, airy rooms and gentle mountain breezes dancing through the trees in the yard. The place had stood empty for a couple of years, and they began renovations soon after moving in. An electrician had been called first to fix the attic light, which kept turning itself on, but to no avail. Even after new wiring, the light continued to come on in the night.

"Guess it's a ghost," Mike had said, and with that it was put on the bottom of the list of things to be fixed.

Mike was working on the guttering when the first real incident happened. Barbara had been reading a "How To" book in the living room when she heard the front door close. She assumed Mike needed some help, and she raised her gaze to ask when she saw a man dressed in a military uniform standing in the entrance foyer. He didn't speak, only looked toward her. She figured it was just a neighbor making a visit. She was upset that he hadn't even bothered to knock, but this was the country, where she was told folks did just drop in without any notice. "Can I help you?" she asked, then watched as the man disappeared into thin air before her eyes.

She couldn't believe what she had seen and attributed the whole thing to being overtired. She didn't mention it to Mike. He wouldn't have believed her anyway, she thought.

Just a few nights later, the twosome was going upstairs to bed, and both Mike and Barbara saw a lady floating on the stairway. After only a moment, she too vanished into nothingness as they stood staring.

Soon afterward, maybe a week or so, a child could be heard crying in different rooms of the house, and a cat was seen on several occasions, sitting between the fire-dogs in the fireplace.

The couple didn't have a cat, and they wondered how a cat could have gotten inside and why it was in the fireplace; but it, too, disappeared upon closer investigation.

Mike and Barbara never felt any fear and believed maybe the ghosts living there were why they got such a good price on the place. Nonetheless, the soldier, the woman, and the cat appearing and disappearing over the months, coupled with the cries of the child, began to play on their nerves.

Nothing ever happened when company was visiting, and some even laughed at the couple when they told their strange tales, saying they were afflicted with "The Clean Mountain Living Disease" and a move back to the city would rid them of all ghostly sights and sounds.

Iris didn't laugh, nor did she make fun of her friends when they told her their stories. She had lived in these mountains all her life, and she knew ghosts did walk here. She had heard their tales since she was a small child on her mother's knee.

She hadn't witnessed these particular ghosts, but she believed what Mike and Barbara told her and had decided maybe the ghosts didn't know they were dead and simply needed to be told and sent on their way.

Mike and Barbara didn't want any part of the exorcism and planned to be away when Iris removed the unwelcome ghosts from their house. Iris had now completed her research. The books she had read were quite clear on the procedures she should follow. Only the priest had warned her to be careful, saying evil, just like good, came in all forms and she could be seriously hurt should her faith waver. He asked the gentle country woman to reconsider, but Iris was determined at least to try to help Mike and Barbara. They were friends and would do the same for her if their situations were reversed.

Night settled, and the darkness thickened. Iris hadn't seen or heard anything and, taking a deep breath, she prayed a silent prayer. Then with a flashlight from her purse, she took the pack from the floor and climbed the stairs to the little eight-foot-by-eight-foot attic room. Once there, she unpacked her bag and unrolled her sleeping bag, placing it in the center of the room between two closets, one on either side. Then she removed the black candle, the silver bell, and her aged, leather-bound Bible.

Then she unzipped a side pocket and took out a little bottle of water the Catholic priest had blessed. She sprinkled it about the room, then sat down on the sleeping bag. She lit the candle, opened the Bible to a specific scripture, and placed the bell at a precise angle to each. She sighed deeply and tried to make herself comfortable to await whatever would come next.

The night grew long and Iris grew tired, yet she was determined to tend to the task before her. So she waited, yet the ghost didn't appear in the candle's glow

A banging on the attic door brought Iris to total wakefulness, and she stumbled the few feet to the door. It was Barbara and Mike. Fearing for their friend, they had returned early to see about her fate. It was six o'clock in the morning.

"I must have fallen asleep," she said to the twosome. "I don't remember lying down or even becoming sleepy."

"Did you see the ghosts?" Mike asked. "Did they come?"

"No. Nothing," she responded. "I'm sorry."

Iris, Mike, and Barbara looked about the room, only to discover the ghost had indeed made a visit. The candle, burned only halfway down, was extinguished; the bell lay on its side; the Bible was closed; and the electric light was turned on and the long pull-cord was wrapped around one of the closet doorknobs and tied securely in a double knot.

SIMPLICITY OF THE MIND

LIZZIE WEBBER WAS WELL INTO HER FIF-
ties when she gave birth to her only son, Tommy. Soon
after his birth, her husband, Eustis, died, leaving the
woman alone to raise her son as best as she could in the
rural reaches of southern Appalachia when times were
bad at best and far worse for Lizzie and her child.

Tommy wasn't like the other children when he was a
small boy. Most folk said he was simple-minded; but as
he grew older, young folk called him just plain crazy the
way he carried on about ghosts and goblins and was so
afraid of the dark.

The old woman and her boy lived in a shack on a
river bottom, long before overfarmed by the owner until
the dirt was too poor to grow anything more than a few
meager root crops for Lizzie and Tommy's own use.

The place where they lived in the North Georgia
mountains had seen bad times. It had seen times of horror, too, and somehow Tommy could still see them. He
saw them when the sun gave way to the moon and the day
slipped into night, and even though his old mama discouraged his ramblings, he told stories of what he had
seen and heard to folks who came to visit the widow and
her son.

The school kids often played impish pranks on Tommy and his mother by throwing rocks on top of the tin roof of their home at night, bringing the boy to tears. He feared the goblins were there to take him away.

The strange stories were known long before Tommy brought them to attention once more; they had just died down over the years. Since the families in many of these stories still lived scattered about the hills, it didn't help to keep them alive. Some things were better off forgotten. Tommy had never known the people or the stories before, yet somehow he could hear the voices calling in the wind at sunset and into the night.

"That little baby cries at the spring, Mama," he said once. "I hear her at night. That little girl that drowned."

"No, Tommy," his mama said. "There's no baby crying. You're just imagining it."

"No, no, Mama," he said. "I heard it. Then the wind cried and now it cries all the time. You can see it blowing and hear it too, all the time. It's calling that little baby."

Lizzie never turned the lights off at night. It seemed to be the darkest of darkness when the daylight left their little shack. It always seemed to throw the boy into some kind of terrified fit when he couldn't see, and Lizzie felt safer too now that she had begun to hear the crying from the spring. She never saw any sign of a child but knew one had mysteriously drowned many years earlier. She noticed the wind, after Tommy mentioned its peculiar blowing, and it did blow in a circular movement all the time. An eeriness was beginning to creep across the old river bottom.

"It felt like something evil was coming back to maybe take anybody living on this land. Maybe it's cursed. I just wanted Tommy away and safe so we moved to town. The only empty house was just another shack near the church cemetery, but we took it anyway. Tommy knew they was dead folk planted over there, but they was supposed to be," the old woman said, sure she had done the right thing as she comforted the big man-child by patting him on the arm.

The old river bottom still remains unfarmed and un-lived on, grown high with pine trees that whirl and twist in a crying wind.

Folks living nearby say they believe Tommy's stories. They, too, have felt something strange shrouding them when they walked down to the river to fish. They say they've heard the crying from the spring and also heard the splashing sound of perhaps a child falling into the water.

Maybe the ghosts did call out to Tommy, seeing per-haps another life to join them, or maybe Tommy called out to them in his lonely simple-mindedness.

Nancy's Wake

RACHAEL AND SARAH LOOKED SOFTLY IN on their brother-in-law where he lay in the back bedroom. They knew he was only pretending to sleep, but they did not disturb him as he was not in any shape to be sociable.

Their sister Nancy was dead since yesterday evening, laid out in her best clothes in the upstairs bedroom, the one right over the kitchen stove. Even though everyone knew it was coming, nobody was prepared for her to die. Her husband, Arthur Branham, was taking it worse than anybody, especially after the terrible fright he'd had in the garden last night.

"How is Arthur?" asked their mother, Martha Hutchison, when Rachael and Sarah went back to the kitchen. Many of their neighbors had gathered this evening for Nancy's wake, and Martha was surrounded by friends.

"He might have been dozing," replied Rachael. "He didn't say anything."

"Him and Nancy sure had a bad year," said Cloy Jones, who lived closest, right across the cornfield. "Most Sundays he didn't even have a congregation big enough to preach to, with so many gone to fight for the Yankees from around here, and others give up on farmin' and moved to Knoxville. And then Nancy had to take the TB."

"Sure is a shame," said another neighbor.

"My George says this land's gettin' too poor to farm," said Cloy.

Another neighbor, Emma, said to Rachael, "It's just a pity your sister Mary got took with the tuberculosis while she was down in Knoxville nursin' them soldiers back in '66."

"Well," Rachael said, "Nancy loved Mary best of all us Hutchisons. She didn't want anybody else to tend her when she took sick."

"It wasn't but a few months after Mary died that we knowed Nancy'd tuk it too," said Mrs. Hutchison mournfully, wiping a tear away with her apron. "I reckon more's died of disease after the war than has died by fightin'."

Rachael sighed. Tomorrow they would lay Nancy alongside Mary in the old Snodderly Cemetery behind the barn, where all her mama's people and her daddy Maston's, too, waited for the Last Great Day.

Rachael didn't care much for sitting down with all the neighbors in her mama's kitchen, but they'd brought enough food with them for three days, and the best table was already laid and tea brewed, so she thought it was okay to catch her breath. She was satisfied that they had laid Nancy out upstairs all fancy and right and proper respectable. The menfolk were prowling the garden, talking with her dad about the tobacco crop, except for Arthur, of course. She only wished there hadn't been such a ruckus kicked up last night when Nancy died.

"Well, tell me, now," said Cloy Jones suddenly, as if she'd read Rachael's mind. "I've heard something right queer about last night. Arthur Branham was tellin' my George something about noises and white things!"

Rachael sighed and wished Arthur Branham hadn't been telling.

There was a bump above them on the floor above the big kitchen. None of the ladies noticed, as they waited for

Rachael to tell the story, glad that Cloy had had the nerve to ask since they all wanted to know. She hesitated, remembering, reluctant to satisfy their curiosity.

Nancy had had a real low day yesterday, and the family figured it wouldn't be much longer that she'd be suffering. Martha was waiting beside Nancy's bed, Rachael and Sarah were in the kitchen, and Maston and the boys were finishing the evening chores in the barn. It was nearly dusk.

Arthur Branham had been walking in agitation around and around the back yard for some time, thinking about his lonesome future without Nancy. Of course, she'd been a fine, faithful wife, given to good works and strong opinions as most Appalachian women were, visiting the poor and widowed, comforting the afflicted, and full of Christian virtue. She may have visited Fannie Elder on the other side of Loyston too often to suit him, paying attention as he did to the rumors of nightly goings-on at her shack in the woods. Fannie worried him; she was Cherokee and knew about the old medicines and didn't hesitate to use them. Nancy had asked for her many times this past week, but he'd refused. A preaching man had his reputation to consider.

As Arthur had reflected on these things, there came a cry from Mother Martha in the upstairs window, and he knew Nancy had drawn her last breath. But that was not all he heard. A low moaning—no, more a rumbling groaning—seemed to come from deep within the old house that had sheltered Nancy all her childhood days, an animal sound, without words, an inarticulate language of loss and pain and dismay as if there were an entity that defied Death his evening's harvest, or perhaps one that celebrated the taking.

Even as Arthur's mind rocked from these utterings, his eyes surely deceived him also. For there, beyond the hollyhocks—what were those white, fluid movements that floated just above the ground? Back and forth across the lawn they drifted, now clustering together, now breaking asunder, among the zinnias, behind the cabbage, around the sycamore. Arthur fell to his knees—or perhaps they gave way—and began to pray mightily for his deliverance.

Rachael and her sisters also had heard the unearthly sounds from here in this familiar kitchen. Yet now, the next day, she still hesitated to tell her neighbors about it, her practical nature struggling to repress her primitive fear. Believing in ghosts just wasn't civilized. As the ladies watched her, waiting, another bump, this one louder, came again from the ceiling. Startled from her thoughts, Rachael looked about her. "Has Sarah gone back upstairs?" she asked.

"I'm right here," her sister answered from beside the stove.

"Perhaps Arthur has gone up to—" began her mother, but she was interrupted. Creeping into their ears came a low moan, a hair-raising groan, as a person coming to consciousness after a long illness, a dry-throated, un-formed croaking. It could be heard in the eastern corner above them, coming down to the south, now turning as it reached the wall, now going west, moving slowly, a low sobbing groan—the ladies had forgotten to breathe. They looked into each other's eyes, aghast. Then with one will they moved toward the kitchen door and toward the back porch, their terror rising as screams in their throats.

One voice rang above the tumult. "What's everyone afraid of?" called Rachael, though she trembled herself. The ladies stopped, embarrassed at their nerves. "It's only a sound. It can't hurt you."

The ladies looked at each other. None wanted to be considered cowardly by her neighbors. They began to murmur excuses to each other, slowly regathering around the table. But they were cut short again by a louder voice that came above their own, a voice with no countenance.

"I may not hurt you," it said darkly, "but I am going to show myself to you on the corner of the kitchen table!" The ladies gasped and drew back, clutching at each other. "And I may scare you to death!"

They could not think. They simply ran for safety, their terror rising once again from constricted throats as screams of denial. Their husbands came rushing, but could find nothing. There was no one in the kitchen, no one in the hall. They held their wives until they stopped sobbing.

Rachael, with typical Appalachian strength, gathered her shawl and her courage about her and marched upstairs to the best bedroom, where Nancy lay. Her sister looked peaceful, lying ready for her coffin tomorrow, undisturbed by the hysteria downstairs. Rachael didn't know what to think, but she felt relieved that her sister looked just as she had when they left her earlier that afternoon.

She came back down the stairs to see Arthur. When she knocked and was bidden to come in, she found him sitting on the side of the bed, his head drooping into his hands.

"Oh, Rachael," Arthur moaned pitifully. "What was that awful racket? It sounded like that—thing—in the garden last night."

"I don't know what it was," Rachael answered rather sharply. She had always found Arthur to have more bombast than backbone.

"Has Fannie Elder sent a spirit to take Nancy's—"

"Don't be ridiculous!" she interrupted him. "Why would Fannie do something like that? She's no witch. She's just an old lady who knows about herbs. You should've let her come give Nancy a poultice to ease her sufferin'. You know they'd been friends all their lives. She was callin' for Fannie all week."

"I know," he moaned again. He looked up at her with

red eyes. "I went to see Fannie the day before Nancy died. I told her it wouldn't look right, her tendin' a good Christian woman like Nancy."

"Who's to say Fannie's not Christian herself?" Rachael said angrily. "Just because she's not Baptist—"

"She started muttering in some strange language," Arthur said. "When I left, I could hear her cackling laughter. I think she must have put haunts in this place."

Rachael's practical mind rejected the idea, but she remembered the dark and evil voice in the garden and in the kitchen and was almost inclined to agree with him. She said nothing, however. With another sorrowful look at Arthur's miserable face, she went to set supper on the table for the guests at Nancy's wake.

THE NIGHT THAT
FLETCHER AND
ROSE SPENT

MASTON'S PLACE WAS HAUNTED, AND everybody in the neighborhood knew it. Some said it was because Maston was such an ornery cuss and recollected how Maston had once killed his wife's only milk cow for a family reunion because otherwise he couldn't afford to put meat on his table that weekend. Others said, no, Maston was as sweet to his wife and family as anybody ever could be, and how Mr. Man, his handyman, died of natural causes. Maston had hired him to help Martha while he was off at the war, and Mr. Man had done a right good job. Maston had even buried Mr. Man in the family graveyard, though he never got him a headstone.

Whatever was causing the place to be haunted, it sure was causing George a passel of trouble. He remembered the first time he heard anything from the Hutchisons' place, the night Nancy died. He and his wife had gone up to her wake. Cloy had brought her best biscuits, a chicken dish, and a big spice cake to add to the huge collection of food on the table from the neighbors. He and the other

menfolk had been wandering around in the garden waiting for the ladies to set supper on the table when there
was such a commotion from the kitchen you'd think the
ladies were trying to wake Nancy from the dead, only to
hear them tell it, Nancy or somebody was already awake
from the dead and was scaring them out of their wits.

Since that night, things had never been the same for
Maston and Martha's place. Even after Nancy had been
laid in her grave, the noises from the old house continued. That was how all the talk began, that maybe Maston himself enjoyed all the attention he was getting from
his hauntin' and was keeping up the reputation.

George looked out his front window toward the
Hutchisons', just visible above the young pine growth.
The old house had been empty for years now, Maston and
Martha both lying up beside Nancy and Mary in Martha's
family graveyard, the old Snodderly Cemetery. Yet the
noises continued. Sometimes they woke George and Cloy
from a sound sleep, sometimes they came at midday. The
voices, the groaning and inarticulate deep sounds, could
come from the house at any time of the day or night.
George and Cloy had decided to give it up. He had built a
new place closer to town and had spent his last night
here. Cloy had already gone to the new house that afternoon, but George waited for his brother Fletcher to pay a
call on him. He had a proposition for Fletcher and his
new bride, Rose.

He heard a wagon rumbling up the road, and he took
one last minute to look about his home for the final time.
They'd been real comfortable here, had raised their children successfully enough, and he was sorry to have to go.
But for Cloy's sake, for her frazzled nerves, he'd agreed to
move last year, and he'd be glad for some peace himself
now that their new house was finished. Their kids had
loved all the ruckus from the house next door and had
gone ghost hunting several times, over Cloy's wishes, of

course. But they'd never seen a thing while they were over there.

He opened his front door, expecting to welcome his brother, but the road was empty. In spite of himself, a cold tremor shook his spare frame as the sound of the wagon approached without substance and rumbled noisily past his doorstep. George turned his face as if watching the wagon pass even while his eyes perceived nothing. Even the iron of the harness clinked with the invisible horse's movements, and the wagon clattered on up toward Maston's house. He'd forgotten about that cussed wagon, it had been such a while since its last trip by. The townsfolk insisted it was the wagon of a tinker Maston had taken some sort of dislike to some years back, who had come up this road before George and Cloy lived here and for some reason had never returned. George didn't think Maston would ever have murdered anybody and that the tinker had simply gone on his way by another trail, bypassing Loyston. But you can't convince some folks, and there was no denying that a wagon rolled on this road that nobody could ever see with earthly eyes, and that sometimes you could even hear what might have been pots and pans clanging with the motion of the wheels.

George heard another wagon coming from the direction of town, and he figured that it must be Fletcher and Rose this time. He wondered if he should mention the ghost wagon to them. No, let them find out for themselves. They'd be doing good to get that far in this neighborhood, anyway. The noises would be enough, if they came during the night tonight. George sighed and went to meet his brother and sister-in-law as they rounded the bend to his porch.

"Of course we can do it!" said Rose with her usual spunk later that evening. They sat before a cozy fire though the evening wasn't really cool. "This is a stout house, and sturdy, and we need a place like this. If it was really dangerous, George wouldn't have offered us the place. What're a few noises?"

"Well, I've heard those sounds that come from the Hutchisons'," said her husband, gloomily, "though I didn't know they'd moved here, too. They weren't something you could sleep with." He wasn't at all sure that even his practical, cheery Rose could stand up to a night in this house. He remembered from his childhood, staying with George and Cloy and their children, how frightened he'd been by the clanging and banging, thrashing and moaning emanating from the house across the tobacco field. But they couldn't refuse George's offer without a trial; stay in his house for one night, and the house was theirs. What young couple just starting out wouldn't stand up to a haunting for that bargain?

So now Fletcher didn't really answer his bride, he just gave her a quiet smile of encouragement across the coals and said, "I reckon it's time to turn in."

"I didn't figure exactly to turn in," said Rose with a grin on her round young face. "I don't want no haints catching me in my nightgown. Let's just set here by the fire a while and see what happens."

Fletcher thought about Cloy's freshly aired bed and wished his wife wasn't so determined to best the ghosts. He'd like to try out the bed to see if it suited him. George's wife was a good housekeeper, and Rose had figured there wouldn't be any mice or even droppings in any of the cupboards. They were both thinking of this house rather contentedly, rocking by the low fire, when they were startled upright by an unearthly grinding noise coming from across the field. Rose clutched Fletcher's arm.

"What is it?" she whispered.

He didn't answer as they peered wide-eyed into the darkness toward Maston's old house. The grinding filled the room, even rattling a loose pane in the eastern window. They forgot to breathe, willing the thunderous noise to cease. After a long minute, it did, and they were left in silence, which the crickets and katydids filled, causing them to wonder if the night critters had heard the noise at all or if it was intended only for human ears. Rose relaxed slowly against her chair back, though she still held tightly to Fletcher's arm.

"What do you think?" she asked shakily.

"I don't know. Nothing bad happened in that house, just remember that. Somebody just wants to scare us tonight."

"Nobody murdered or anything?"

"Not that I ever knew about." He patted her soft arm, wishing he'd had the good sense to refuse George's offer.

Rose's eyes twinkled in the firelight. "I knew we shouldn't go to bed."

He was reflecting on how glad he was that he'd married her when they again began to hear banging and slamming from next door, accentuated by groaning and crashes. The noises began softly and slowly crescendoed, seeming to grow closer to them as they increased in volume. "Are they coming here?" Rose asked, brown eyes wide.

For an answer, Fletcher set his jaw and rose from the hearth, with Rose still clutching his arm. Slowly, carrying a lamp before them, they began to roam the house, trembling with each loud crash, cringing at moans nearby, creeping with determination from room to room, expecting at every step to be ambushed by they could not imagine what. The din was so loud they could not communicate, but they took courage from each other's steady grip. Fletcher tried not to let the lamp shake in his hand.

All night they roamed in George's house, searching for any source of the terror, growing more convinced that the crashing, groaning, thumping cacophony was caused by some force undetectable by human eyes, a force their minds could not comprehend, and one with which they could not and did not want to deal. They had been brought up to have a healthy respect for the powers of darkness and believed in them thoroughly. If the haunting was being done by demons, there was only one thing to do.

At dawn the couple was once again before the fireplace that had been so comforting earlier, resting during a lull in the din. Their cheery fire lay in ashes on the hearth, dead and cold like their dreams of happiness in George's house.

"This house is not good for us," Fletcher said to his wife.

"There's evil here!" she agreed, and they jumped as a crashing like two dinner plates breaking sounded just above their heads. "We've stayed too long already!"

They could barely see to find their horse and harness it with haste. They wondered briefly at the animal's calmness, for it was obvious that the unearthly din had not disturbed its slumber at all, but in their anxiety to be away they did not discuss it. As the wagon rolled away, the banging and crashing behind them bade them a horrifying farewell.

After a mile, as the peace of the road soothed them, Rose's tears of regret began to fall. "My mama won't understand why we stayed so long. She wouldn't think any house was worth that scare. I don't intend to say a word about this night."

Fletcher felt surprised, but he patted her cheek in agreement, glad to have her safely away. "We'll just say the house didn't suit us."

Rose kept the secret of that night for the rest of her life. When she was eighty-two and living up north of her old home in Loyston, a young woman called. Seems the area she and Fletcher lived in had been made a state park back in the thirties when Roosevelt was creating all that work for the people who couldn't find jobs. They'd built a dam on the river and called the new lake Norris, and made a park with a smaller lake they called Big Ridge. They'd planted acres and acres of pine seedlings on those worn-out tobacco fields that rose above the water level, to show the people what good management could accomplish. This young woman, who was a naturalist at Big Ridge, wanted to know about Maston's house and George's house. She'd found a relative of the Hutchisons' who was talking about those old haunting stories. She wanted to know if what she heard about the night that Rose and Fletcher spent was true.

Rose was relieved to hear that Maston's and George's homes were no longer there, not covered by the water but gone anyway. She remembered the night in every distinct and terrifying detail, but she wasn't about to admit it at this late date. She told the lady she and Fletcher lived in another house quite happily in the same area, but she'd never lived in George's. She pretended to have no knowledge whatever about its haunting or Maston's. When Rose hung up the phone, she couldn't suppress a chuckle. There'd be no ghost stories around Big Ridge Park if it were up to her.

HARRISON MEETS
AUNT MARY

GEORGE HAD RESIGNED HIMSELF TO HAV-
ing his house stand empty after Rose and Fletcher refused
his offer. When the villagers asked why they were staying with her mother instead of in George's house, they
wouldn't say. George certainly wasn't going to bring the
scary noises that poured around his house to the townspeople's attention again. George could tell by the determined look on Rose's face that she wasn't about to talk
about that night when Maston's ghosts had scared her half
to death, but George could guess what had happened
since he and Cloy had had lots of experience with those
haunting things themselves.

So winter and a spring and a summer had passed
with his house standing empty above the town of Loyston
in the East Tennessee hills. Most of the fall was gone, too,
and now it was time to gather fodder for his stock. George
had planted his corn this year in one of Maston's old
fields that had lain fallow since his death, because his
own fields needed a rest. He'd recruited his younger
brother, Harrison, to help him gather the leaves and stalks

and store them in his barn. Harrison was big and happy and strong and never had much to say. But he knew about the ghost stories that surrounded Maston's old house and George's house, and his practical mind thought they were nonsense; so George figured he was the best one to ask. Fletcher was different, of course, since that night he and Rose spent in George's house. Fletcher had found an excuse to keep from helping George in the corn every day so far, and George figured it was because his house and Maston's lay between his barn and the field. Fletcher wanted no more to do with either house. Harrison, now he could be counted on.

George plodded along the footpath to his barn, his arms full of cornstalks. He had to pass Maston's house and barn to get to his own barn, which was mighty inconvenient, but there wasn't a road for him to use his wagon. Harrison was ahead of him at the barn already. George glanced uneasily toward Maston's old house though he could see only the steep roof gable through the young pines that had grown around it since it had stood empty. He'd been expecting to hear its terrifying noises each time he had approached, but they'd worked all day and the house hadn't yet made any attempt to break the afternoon stillness. He planned to be well away, back to town and in his cozy new home, long before dark. In fact, he carried his last load and was considerably relieved as he rounded the turn past Maston's barn and came abreast of the quiet house.

He couldn't help thinking of the house's dead occupants as he labored with the stalks. So many of them had been claimed by tuberculosis. Aunt Mary, bright of eye and red of hair, who'd died many years ago, after she caught the killer while nursing soldiers in the war; Aunt Nancy, who caught it from nursing her sister Mary and whose wake had started all this haunting stuff. Then their folks Maston and Martha, and who knew who else. As a little boy, George had loved Aunt Mary best, because of her sparkling eyes and the licorice sticks she slipped him during church. He'd missed her for years after she died, and still did, he reflected now. Still, there were lots of Hutchisons left around the Loyston area. In fact, Fletcher had been raised by one of Maston's boys, Big Jim, after his parents took fever.

George sighed toward the house as he passed the back porch and his own barn came into view. He could see the interior, brightened by the lowering sun striking the shining pineboard floors. His eye caught a movement, just a small one, but it caused him to pause. Inside, by the stairs, and close to the big front window, the rocking chair tilted. Its back was toward the west, so the window's sunny glare confused his tired eyes. But he was certain—he was sure it wasn't his imagination—that someone sat there in the rocker. With cornstalks hindering his view, he stepped closer, peering anxiously through the screen and window. No question—the chair rocked because a woman sat in it, dressed in the long skirt of a past decade, her hair—did it glint red in the sun?—piled high atop her head. She seemed to rest her head against the chair back; but George thought he saw an uncommon light reflected in her eyes, though her gaze was not directed toward him. George recognized her with a shock, and the stalks crashed down at his boots.

"Aunt Mary," he whispered. His heart registered the truth even while his mind rejected it—the figure rocking could be no other person. She was just as he remembered her as a boy before she had sickened and died. Why was she here, rocking in her father's house in her chair by the window on this quiet afternoon in the fall?

George knew that after all these haunting years, a figure from beyond the grave was here before his eyes. He turned and fled as fast as he could toward his barn, calling in terror for Harrison. Hearing ghostly noises was one thing, but seeing a dead person was beyond his endurance.

"Harrison!" he yelled. "Harrison!"

His brother's call startled Harrison so much that he dumped his work and sprinted to the door of the barn. He'd never heard his brother with such a tone in his voice, even though over the years they'd been afraid before, living with haints the way they did. Harrison had heard the noises, too, in the past, but had always laughed them off as the pranks of neighboring boys.

He wasn't inclined to laugh now, however, at the sight of George's face. White-skinned, eyes staring, George clutched at Harrison's sweaty shirt.

"Aunt M-Mary!" George stuttered, pointing back. "In the rocker! In Maston's house!"

Harrison shook his head in denial. "Not possible, George. Dead for years."

"Yes, I saw her in front of the west window."

Harrison had plenty of faith in his brother but none whatever in hauntings. He said, "I'll look," and strode off down the path, leaving George to sink upon a log and mop his sweating face.

With more than a little anger toward the intruder who had given his brother such a fright, Harrison grabbed the back-door handle without hesitation. A glance inside, which was still lit brightly by the setting sun, confirmed George's claim, and Harrison was quite surprised. There was indeed a woman sitting there in the old family rocker. Harrison had seen a tintype of his Aunt Mary as a young girl, and this slightly older lady did fit the picture. Amazed, but not frightened, Harrison determined to speak with her. He yanked the door handle. At least, he attempted to yank the handle. Harrison found that his arm had no power and his feet could not go forward. He thought, *I am not afraid of this figure in the chair, but I cannot move.* For a long moment he struggled strongly against whatever power held him motionless on the porch, and during that time the lady turned her bright eyes on his face and gave him a warm and loving smile.

Caught in that gaze, Harrison ceased his struggle.

Slowly he let go of the handle and began to back from the door. As he shifted his position, the sun was screened by an evening cloud bank on the horizon so that the room's light faded quickly and turned a dim gray. He could no longer see her.

He walked slowly to George at the barn, who looked at him anxiously. "Yes, she was there," Harrison said. "She smiled at me."

Harrison changed just a little while later. His fine strength ebbed, the color left his ruddy cheeks, his flesh hung slackly on his bones. The family knew from the first it was tuberculosis and they were full of anger and regret at his going. But Harrison just remembered Mary's smile and never had much to say.

Maston's House
Takes Another

JIMMY WAS FEELING VERY UPSET, ONLY HE didn't want his folks to see it. So he wandered the hills above the Loyston village to avoid going down to supper. He knew these paths, hollows, and hills better than any other boy around, though probably not as well as his uncle Harrison had, but he was dead now and didn't count. Uncle George, old and in his chair by the fire, liked to tell him and the other young 'uns stories about his old house and his great-grandaddy Maston's being haunted. George even had to build his wife a new house down in Loyston, the racket from ghosts had gotten so bad. Jimmy didn't know whether to believe those stories or not. He'd been in that old house of Maston's lots of times and had never heard a ghost, or seen one. Jimmy thought that was probably too bad. He thought he'd be pretty brave if he did ever meet up with one.

Jimmy was usually a light-hearted boy, living as he did in the country and close to the Smoky Mountains, where there was plenty of room to have a dog and raise some food. His father had been killed in the Argonne

Forest, and his mother had been taken by the influenza epidemic, but that was years ago, and Jimmy lived with his brother and his brother's wife. They were happier now that the war was over, though Jimmy was tired of hearing people discuss Wilson's plan that Congress wouldn't have anything to do with. That wasn't what was making him upset, though, on this quiet afternoon. It was Esther.

Esther's family lived in his great-grandaddy Maston's old house, and had for a while. Her father was a grandson of Maston and so had a right to live there. Esther was quite a bit younger than he, but she was always cooking up some mischief that Jimmy really enjoyed, and they would let her brothers in on it too, if they asked nicely and did her chores that night. Once they had sat on Maston's sunken grave and called to see if he would come up. Another time they had dissolved cayenne pepper in her mother's soup beans while she was outside and spoiled the entire meal that night. They had laughed about that for weeks.

Lately, though, Esther had not been as lively and couldn't come out to play much. He'd gone up to their house every day or so and was always told she was too sick. This morning at breakfast, Jimmy had caught his brother and his wife, Dewey and Elizabeth, exchanging that look grown-ups use when they don't want to discuss something important with children. Elizabeth had just asked what he was going to do that day.

"Reckon I'll go see how Esther is," he'd replied as he had every day for the past month.

Then he saw the look. It was a sad look between Dewey and Elizabeth across the table and not meant for him, only it told him everything he didn't want to know.

"What," he said. "Tell me what's wrong with her. Is she going to die?"

Dewey wiped his mustache and said, "They sent for the doctor last night, Jimmy. Looks like Esther has tuberculosis."

103

So Jimmy wandered the hills in sorrow and in anger, wishing that it did not have to be, for he knew all the family before him who had died of that disease. For nearly eighty years Hutchisons had been dying too young of tuberculosis. He knew he could do nothing to stop her dying; he thought his anger might be big enough and powerful enough to keep her here. What if her spirit, like those of the others before her who died in that house, could not rest? Jimmy didn't think he could stand it if Esther became a haunt, too.

When he finally returned to the house, it was almost dark, and Dewey and Elizabeth weren't there, though his supper sat warm on the back of the cookstove. He ate it, lonely, and went to bed right away.

Dewey and Elizabeth were walking up to Maston's house to see if they could do anything for Esther's family. They hadn't planned on going so late, but they were holding supper for Jimmy, and when he didn't come by dark, they lit their lantern and set out.

"Do you reckon Jimmy will be okay when Esther dies?" Elizabeth asked quietly as they walked along. "They've been mighty good friends."

"Yeah, he'll grieve but forget after a while," Dewey said. He remembered when Harrison had died and how upset he'd been, but he had felt better after a year or so.

"You know, I don't think I'd want to live in Maston's house," Elizabeth remarked, stepping carefully across a rippling creek on stones some long-ago farmer had set there. "Too much sickness, all that TB. Too many scary stories."

"Been quiet the last few years, though," Dewey said. "Old house must be losing its haints."

"Well, that'd sure be nice," Elizabeth answered rather drily.

They came into sight of the house, set on a rise above the footpath with the hill continuing up behind it, and were startled as a commotion began in the brush behind them. Some sort of animal was coming toward them at a rapid rate; they stopped, and Dewey raised his lantern in curiosity. Surely it wasn't a night critter, a fox or an opossum; they were smart enough to stay away from folk. Had to be a lost dog looking for a friendly face. The running noises, leaves rustling, and branches shuffling approached them quickly where they stood at the edge of the yard, but they could not yet see anything. Elizabeth expected an exuberant stray to jump out, so noisily and rapidly did it approach. She braced her slender legs for the weight of the unseen animal, but though the noises were now upon them, the light of the lantern revealed nothing.

Suddenly, Elizabeth and Dewey were shoved by an invisible force that felt like a dog at their legs, running around them, between their feet, whipping around the yard close by as dogs will when they are excited. Elizabeth clutched at Dewey's arm to steady herself and gasped, "What is it?" But he was attempting to keep the lantern upright in his hand and could not answer.

"Git!" he addressed the unseen with considerable frustration, the lantern swinging wildly as they both peered around themselves while struggling to stay on their feet. He took her arm strongly. "Let's get up to the house!"

In the dark they could still hear the dog, or whatever it was, running back and forth, and it grazed their calves and knees several times, causing them to stumble and hurry. Even when they reached the house, where lamp-light from the windows threw pools of welcome illumination onto the ground outside, they could not see this unknown animal. At the steps, it left them.

Dewey and Elizabeth paused a minute to catch their breath. "More of Maston's foolishness," muttered Dewey, looking closely at Elizabeth to see if she was still fit for a

visit with Esther's folks. "I reckon we spoke too soon."
She was pale but more concerned about the sickness of
Esther than about the haints. She just shook her head.
People in these parts had all grown up aware of the
goings-on at Maston's. The house had been behaving
pretty well in recent years; too bad if the hauntings were
starting up again.

"Let's just not say anything," Elizabeth said. "They've
got enough trouble right now."

And the family did indeed have trouble, for just that
evening, while Dewey and Elizabeth walked to Maston's,
while the unseen dog had cavorted and bumped them,
the little girl Esther had died.

Jimmy was back at Esther's house, only she was not
there any longer. His little friend with the big brown
eyes and long dark hair was lying in a pine box in the
old Snodderly graveyard behind Maston's house, where
they'd put her this afternoon. It was no comfort whatever
to Jimmy that Esther no longer suffered or that she was
buried in peace with her great-grandmother and Uncle
Harrison and Aunt Mary and Aunt Nancy and all the
other Hutchisons under the trees on the hill. Those were
things that grown-ups told children so they'd stop being
sad. Jimmy didn't think he'd ever stop being sad, and he
didn't intend to try.

It was time to get some sleep. They'd sat all afternoon
together after Esther's burial, the townspeople from Loyston and the farmers from the hills talking about things
that had nothing to do with Esther. Jimmy had heard
again all the stories about this house being haunted, and
he wasn't too excited about staying here all night, especially since Esther wasn't here anymore. He sighed and
turned over in the bed. How had he gotten stuck sleeping
up here in the attic all alone when his cousins were all
downstairs cuddled in beds together?

Dewey and Elizabeth, the last to retire, also thought about Esther and about sleeping in the house. They wouldn't have considered it, except that Esther's mother was in terrible shape and needed extra attention and probably would for some time. The house was very quiet after they were settled, for everyone had been asleep some time before Dewey and Elizabeth went to bed. It wasn't long before they, too, were drifting off to sleep, exhausted like Jimmy from the day's events. Dewey began to snore softly.

There came then, across the still mountain air, a little sound, the barest and tiniest sound of crying in the night, a gentle sobbing sound. Elizabeth felt her drowsiness recede as she listened closely for its direction, thinking about which child it could be who could not sleep for grief. She nudged Dewey awake and said, "Listen. Someone's crying."

He lit the lamp without being asked because he was a kind man and knew Elizabeth would have to check. So they began to slip from room to room, checking on each group of children, who all seemed to be sleeping soundly. They even peered closely at little faces for teartracks, in case a tender heart did not want to discuss its crying and was only pretending to sleep.

As they ascended the attic stairs to see about Jimmy, for it could be no one else since all the others slept, they realized that the crying had never altered nor faded as they went from room to room. Opening a door did not increase the volume; closing a door did not lessen it. The sound was without doubt a child's sobbing, not in anger or in pain but in profound sadness and grief, the sadness that cannot subside with time and loving care.

Elizabeth and Dewey bent over Jimmy's still form, awash in moonlight from the garret window. As they had approached his bed, the sobbing had at last grown louder; but Jimmy was breathing evenly, fast asleep. The window

107

was open to the night breeze; they saw that it was a north window and opened toward the cemetery. If all the children slept, the weeping had to be coming from the cemetery. They looked at each other in the near-dark, frightened indeed. Dewey turned out his lamp so that the moonlight brightened as they crept to the window and leaned out. Elizabeth decided that the sobbing emanated from Esther herself—yet, how could it be?—for Dewey could see Elizabeth's tears of fright and sympathy on her cheeks. Esther, weeping for her lost young life. They stood there shivering, listening.

"Maybe it's another kid gone up to the cemetery to see the grave," whispered Dewey to comfort her. "Some-one from town."

"If it was, we couldn't hear it so good," she answered, and that was true. The crying seemed now to fill the house with its gentle sorrow, though the graveyard was several hundred yards through the woods. No human crying could have been heard from that distance.

As the truth they dreaded spread through their minds, Dewey and Elizabeth realized that Maston's house did not rest as they had hoped, and maybe neither did Maston or the other dead Hutchisons. They grasped hands firmly and in the dark made their way back to their room. As quietly as they could, they pushed a heavy dresser against the door, put a bench upon it, and a quilt rack on top of that.

"This is stupid," hissed Dewey. "If Aunt Mary or somebody wants to come in here, they'll just show up. Furniture against the door won't help."

"Well, if it's not a ghost," said Elizabeth, "this fur-niture will help!"

So all night they kept their vigil while the weeping from the cemetery waxed and waned but never stopped. If only they had known that Jimmy, too, had been awakened, they would have braved any ghost or noise to go to his comfort. But Jimmy, who at their visit lay so peacefully asleep, had been startled by a bump from their furniture moving and had immediately heard the crying and known it was Esther. All night he crouched in terror under his covers, alternately crying, too, and blaming himself for not being brave enough to go to the cemetery to see if he could do anything to comfort her. His daytime mind rejected the ghosts and knew that she was dead and in her box and that was all there was to it. But his nighttime mind, tired and full of Maston stories, was terrified.

In the morning, just at dawn, the whole house was astir, and the smell of biscuits, steak, eggs, and coffee was never more welcome. The family gathered with relief at the table. "We didn't sleep well," admitted one of Esther's aunts to another. Esther's mother was haggard and shook her head sadly.

"I thought I heard crying all night long," said an uncle rather hesitantly, hoping he'd not been the only one.

"Did you hear the crying, Jimmy?" asked Elizabeth, knowing by his peaked face and hollow eyes that he, too, had been awake. She wished he'd called to her.

But he answered boldly, "What crying? Who was crying? If there was crying, why didn't anybody check?" and looked at his relatives around the table.

Everyone looked uncomfortable except for Dewey and Elizabeth. "We did check. We saw that everybody was asleep, including you," answered Dewey gently.

"I didn't hear a thing," said the boy, too ashamed to admit that he'd not had the courage to go to the crying child's comfort, Esther or not.

"We heard it," said another uncle bravely, "and it scared us to death. Maston's ghosts, from the graveyard."

"We piled up our furniture against the door," said the aunt. "We didn't sleep a wink."

"We didn't, either," answered Dewey. "Jimmy—"

"I did hear it!" he blurted and jumped up from his chair. "It had to be Esther. Why can't anybody who dies around here just die? Why do they all have to be noisy and come back and scare everybody? I hate this house! The dead don't rest here! I'll be glad when this house is gone!"

It took a few more years, but Maston's house is gone now, just as Jimmy wished. Esther's family moved on, leaving Maston's house lonely and deserted, by itself in the crowding woods. No one ever cared to live there again.

The country fell on hard times between the wars, and Roosevelt's government looked around for ways to help. The Appalachian foothills seemed a good place to start, worn out by so many years of farming, eroded by the rains, flooded by the torrents in the spring. The people of Loyston were told one day that they would be paid to move to another place, as the old valleys would soon be under the waters of the new Norris Dam, built by the Tennessee Valley Authority, which had been given the task of making their hills green and productive again. So they moved, and some of their homes were covered with the waters of Norris Lake; but their new ones were lighted by electricity, and after they were used to it they didn't mind so much, having to move.

The waters didn't reach up the hill to the Snodderly Cemetery, so Maston's grave is still sunk in the hills of East Tennessee, included in TVA's Big Ridge Park, which was built so the people could play among Jimmy's and Harrison's hills. One of his great-grandsons, Paul, after the park was created, filled the grave with new soil; but it is sunken still. Maston's house, too, has fallen back into the earth, a mound and a memory, the subject of campfire tales on dark summer nights, making children shiver.

But the place of those ghostly doings remains, for the southern hills do not give up their legends easily. Coon dogs brightly pursuing their prey shy up near the Snodderly Cemetery and refuse to continue the chase. Lights once framed by the windows of George's and Maston's homes still sometimes shine through the pine forest planted by the workers in the thirties. Hikers in the area are still sometimes amazed by a dog's whining or perhaps a child's crying from the graveyard, or are surprised by sudden violent storms in the woods near the homes.

The ancient hills know the secrets of Maston's family. The lakes reflect the starshine that Aunt Mary and Harrison, Esther, George, and Jimmy knew. The old pines sigh with their laughter and their tears. Now their spirits seem to rest, and Big Ridge Park guards them with serenity.

Adventure Seekers

SOME TWENTY YEARS AGO, SAMUEL CLAYton, a young man who lived in the North Georgia mountains, and his cousin, Mark Otis, who was visiting from the mountains of northeast Tennessee, rambled about a small town in the Appalachian foothills trying to replace their Saturday night boredom with some excitement or adventure. The town had no movie theater, skating rink, or general teen hangouts, so the twosome decided to check out a few of the back roads. Some were newly graveled or black-topped. Others were still just hard-packed red clay.

Somewhere around ten o'clock that warm, mid-summer night, Sam pulled his old Ford into a small country church cemetery. The gravestones stood like white, aged soldiers, all standing at attention on the dark grassy hillside. The moon was a mere crescent slit in the ever-darkening sky. Wind whooshed leaves from a nearby wood across the ground, making eerie sounds across the mounded graves that marked the resting places of the dead.

"Maybe we shouldn't be here," Mark said to his cousin as Sam turned the car's engine and lights off and opened the door.

"Why not?" Sam asked. "I don't see anybody here to

tell us we can't. Besides, this place is as lively as any-where else we've been tonight. Come on. Always wanted to check out a graveyard at night."

Sam laughed a carefree laugh and gave a scary little "Oooooh" as Mark opened the passenger door and joined his cousin in the dark. A shiver ran through him, and he wished Sam wasn't the adventurous type and they could just go back to Grandma's house and play some cards and listen to the radio.

The twosome strolled amid the marble headstones. Sam ran his fingers over some of the carved letters, trying to identify the names on several of the monuments. Most were so old and weathered by time and the elements there were barely any indentations left.

The moon had swiftly vanished as storm clouds crept over the sky and mashed down on the North Georgia mountains like a heavy hand. Thunder rumbled deep and low in the distance, but Sam paid no mind to the weather and continued to move higher up the hill of the cemetery and further away from the car.

"Hey, Sam," Mark mumbled, hopping over a nearby headstone. "We better make tracks. Storm's moving in fast."

Sam didn't respond to Mark but hurried to the top of the hill where a lone grave stood. The big stone marker looked impressive, towering over those dotted up and down the hillside.

Mark was soon beside Sam. "Look at this," he said, noting a thick haze forming and hovering over the grave.

"Fog?" Sam remarked, his tone a bit shaky.

"It's not fog," Mark said. "Not like any I've ever seen. It's just over this grave, and it's thick. I can't even see through it. Too thick to be fog."

Mark wanted to run away but found his feet wouldn't move. "What is happening here?" he asked in a half-whisper.

"Must be some kind of ghost or maybe a graveyard spirit," Sam answered. "Maybe we better be going." He could hardly catch a breath, and his heart hammered in his chest. His feet remained steadfast to the ground beneath him.

As the two boys stood in sheer terror, a glass case centered in the base of the headstone began to glow through the haze. An open Bible lay inside the case. Instantly, the pages began to turn as if a whirlwind was caught inside the glass box.

Sam felt his legs tingle, and he raised his eyes from the goings-on atop the grave to meet Mark's. Mark's terrified look screamed to be away from this place, this place of hovering smoky haze, glowing glass cases, Bibles with flying pages, and dark so heavy it almost hurt.

"Go," Sam said real low.

Before Mark could speak, lightning thrust its jagged spears across the black sky, lighting the cemetery in an eerie, blue-white brightness.

Both boys ran as if the fingers of death were reaching out to claim them. Jumping gravestones and toppling flowerpots, they raced down the hill.

Neither boy spoke as they clambered inside the safety of the vehicle and locked the doors tight. Sam started the old car and slung gravel over nearby gravestones in his hurry to be gone.

The night seemed to howl in anger. Neither boy slept that night but waited for morning, hoping the storm that surely rose from the cemetery would pass with the coming of daylight.

With the night's passage the storm did stop. The thunder became silent, the lightning abated, the rains stopped, and the roaring wind stilled. It was like any other summer day after a night of storms in the Appalachian foothills, or so it appeared.

Midmorning found the two young men, still shaken

from the previous night, back at the small country cemetery. They righted the toppled flowerpots and fixed the plastic flowers back as best they could, then walked wearily to the top of the hill where the towering gravestone stood guard over the smaller ones dotting the green, grassy hillside. The strange heavy mist was gone, and so was the glowing light and the Bible with its fast-turning pages. Only a sealed empty glass case centered in the base of the headstone atop the grave remained where they had seen it the night before.

"Where'd it go?" Sam asked.

"The Bible?" Mark asked.

The boys stood in wonder. They both knew it had been there the night before, and now it wasn't. There was no answer, and each decided it might be easier not to talk about the experience anymore. They turned and made their way back down the hill as a strange wind picked up from the nearby wood and began to whoosh the wet leaves across the mounded graves marking the resting places of the dead. It made an eerie sound, sending a cold chill through the boys, and they shivered in spite of the warm, sunny day.

THE HAUNTED RED BARN

RIGHT AFTER WORLD WAR I, HANK STAN-field built a red barn. It was big and roomy, and folks around southern Pickens County looked on with interest as the barn neared completion. Finally the day arrived, and the last coat of red paint went on the barn's side. When the animals refused to enter Hank's new barn, it soon became apparent that all was not well.

Someone said, "It's just the wet paint; when it's dry, they'll go in." About a week later Hank was up against it. No farm animal would go into the new red barn. During the day cats and dogs would go in, but as soon as nightfall came, they tore out of the barn as if the Devil himself was after them.

Hank tried an experiment. He brought the farm animals in during the day. They stayed until nightfall, then tore out to the pasture and would not come back.

Around this time folks started saying that the red barn was haunted. However, no reason could be given for the haunting. It was new; nobody had been killed there; there were no suspicious odors—no reason at all.

Finally, Hank's cousin, Jerald Stanfield, from Gilmer County, came down to Pickens and announced he would

116

spend the night in the new barn. "Can't be nothing in there that will scare me," Jerald said.

So at dusk Jerald Stanfield went into the barn with a bedroll. The next morning at daybreak Hank and his neighbors opened the barn door. Nothing. No Jerald, just his bedroll. Jerald Stanfield showed up back home two days later and announced he had joined the Army. He would not talk about what did, or did not, happen that night in Hank's barn.

The Harley twins were the next to stay in the barn, and when the door was opened the next morning, both were gone. They wrote to their folks often—both married in Alabama—but neither ever came home again.

Nobody's fool, Hank used the barn for storage and built another for the livestock. During the day the barn was like any other, but at night it seemed to send off an aura of dread. So for a few years the barn stood as the day it was built—neat, bright—but no living thing ever spent a night there.

About ten years after the barn was built, a stranger came to Hank's farm. He was a feature writer for a national magazine and had been vacationing at one of the mountain lodges when he heard about Hank's barn and the supposed curse on it. This fellow was a recognized war correspondent—no hot-blooded boy or local tough—and covered all kinds of big stories.

At dusk that night, with a manual typewriter, a bottle of whisky, and three packs of cigarettes, the famed reporter entered the red barn of Hank Stanfield.

The next morning at daybreak half the county was in Hank's yard. They were a quiet crowd, and many were sure the journalist would soon emerge. He didn't. So Hank opened the barn door. All was calm. There sat a half empty bottle of whisky, the typewriter, and a burning cigarette. But no living thing was in the barn.

The reporter went on to an even more illustrious career, covering wars in foreign lands, but he never came back. If you get Hank on a good day, he will take you into the barn. You can see the typewriter, the half empty whisky bottle, and the cigarette ash. No one else has tried to stay a night in the barn, and no one has any answer for the strange hauntings of Hank's red barn.

Hank's grandson Earl now runs the farm. Early on, Earl put a padlock on the barn and no longer lets anyone in—or to stay overnight. And although the barn was built more than seventy years ago, it looks as if it had been finished this very day.

STEADFAST STAIN OF DEATH

DEATH BY ACCIDENT HAS ALWAYS BEEN around, but as time passes the victim and the place of the accident are usually forgotten and only a gravestone somewhere indicates the passage of yet another life.

One particular place in southern Appalachia that claimed a young girl's life refuses to be forgotten and continues to display the stains of a life that unfortunately slipped into the next realm many years ago.

Her name was Ellen Brothers, and the claim is that the girl, about sixteen years old, having completed all her daily chores, had come to this place to meet her sweetheart. The young man, Tom Rogers, also about sixteen, had come to tell the girl he had fallen in love with someone else.

It's told that upon hearing his words, the girl lost her footing, slipped, and fell, hitting her head on a huge gray-white stone, and died from her injuries.

A couple traveling through North Georgia, savoring the beauty found in the world's oldest mountains, happened unknowingly upon the place of the tragic accident.

They saw a large, red stain blotting a beautiful gray-white stone, and with water from their cooler, the couple cleaned the stain away.

Proud of their accomplishment and fascinated by the stone's natural beauty, they returned a few days later. The stain had returned, glaring its ugly red mark in the bright afternoon sun. The couple cleaned the stain off again and hoped the stain prankster would not mar nature's goodness anymore.

Late summer rains began, and the couple found sightseeing difficult and decided to travel elsewhere, perhaps farther north. The twosome later made one more trip to the huge stone that had intrigued them so. They heard the sorrowful tale of the young girl from nearby residents who had been out for a walk.

The bloody red stain had returned yet again to scream out in silence from the huge, cool, gray-white stone, in southern Appalachia where death by accident was and is always around.

OUT OF THE MOUTHS
OF BABES

A WOMAN NAMED MARY, A DESCENDANT
with long roots in southern Appalachia, tells a story of
some years past when she was a military wife and her
daughter, Sandi, was only four years old.

"Granny was bad sick," Mary says, "and Sandi and I
had come over from Memphis. The doctor didn't know
whether I should stay on or not."

The elderly woman had been sick for awhile, and
Mary and her daughter had come home to help the family
as needed. Just being close at hand had strengthened the
family's bonds in the time of their present troubles.

Mary decided that if she went home, she could return later, and it was possible for the aged woman to live
quite awhile in her present state. The stroke had left her
paralyzed, but her heart was strong.

Mary called her husband, Billy, telling him she and
Sandi would be coming home on Monday. "Why not Sunday?" he asked.

She didn't know. She had no answer. Mary only
knew they weren't supposed to leave on Sunday morning,
and the only bus left at 7:30 A.M.

Billy drove over from Memphis on Saturday night, knowing his wife needed him beside her. Everyone was glad to have him there, even for only a few hours, and his presence did lift the cloud of gloom surrounding everyone. It was decided Billy, Mary, and Sandi would return home the next day around noon after Billy and Mary had talked with the doctor during his morning rounds.

Mary and her mother, Mable, prepared Sunday morning breakfast. Sandi desperately pleaded for Grandma Mable to go home with her.

Grandma Mable told her granddaughter she couldn't, saying she had to stay and help care for Sandi's great granny.

The little girl was insistent. "No, you don't," Sandi protested. "Great Granny don't need you anymore."

Grandma Mable was distressed by the girl's remarks and said, "Yes, Sandi, dear, she does. Don't you remember going to the hospital to visit? Can't you remember how very sick Great Granny was?"

Sandi replied, "Yes. But she's not there anymore."

Grandma Mable hugged her granddaughter tight and tried to soothe the little girl's agitation.

When the family sat down to breakfast, word came that Great Granny had died.

"I asked when she died," Mary said, "and was told about 8:00 A.M. It was the same time Sandi told my mama that Great Granny didn't need her anymore."

Mary shook her head and said in a low tone, "Mama said I did almost the same thing when I was about three years old." The woman continued, telling the story told to her over the years by her mother.

Mary and her mother enjoyed playing name games, and in one such game sometime in the spring of 1944 Mary asked her mother how many brothers and sisters she had and what all their names were.

"Now Mama had five brothers," Mary said. "And

they were all in the military, and it was wartime. All Mama's brothers were off fighting World War II."

Mary's mama began to name her brothers, but when she came to her brother Paul, the little girl quickly spoke up, saying, "He don't count anymore."

A week later a telegram arrived announcing that Mary's uncle Paul had been killed in action during the Normandy Invasion.

RACHEL

Aunt Rachel, two days after her one hundred and second birthday, entered the small mountain hospital for the last time. She had never married. Her pure white hair barely covered her pink scalp, and her eyes, round and protruding, stared off into the distance.

Rachel had been adopted. She was found near a cave on Sassafras Mountain by the Stanhouse family. They tried to find her kin but never did. So she always said she didn't know who she really was. She was a young girl when they found her, about fifteen, and she didn't remember anything about her life before that.

The following story was told to the family after Rachel's death. The story was told by Nurse Smith and has become a mountain legend.

Rachel opened her eyes and said, "Nurse Smith, I want to tell you a story about my early days."

Nurse Smith listened as Rachel told her about the mountain cave, then her face lit up. "Oh, Nurse, I remember. Oh, God. I'm remembering everything. I know my past."

The nurse checked Rachel's pulse. It was racing, but Rachel had to tell her story.

"Nurse, I see a golden youth. He is holding my hand. Although it is daylight, the sky is darkening. The earth is trembling. The youth is grabbing me, pulling me down, pushing me into a cave.

"The youth said, 'Tara, stay here, my darling. I'll come back for you even if it takes eons of time.'

"I said, 'Oh, Brian,' and the ground shook, and I tumbled down into the cave."

The bell in the reception room rang, announcing a visitor. Nurse Smith walked out into the reception area and saw a golden youth. That was the only way she could describe him.

"Hello," a soft voice said. "I would like to see Rachel Stanhouse."

Nurse Smith pointed and said, "Rachel is in room six."

"Thank you," he said and walked into Rachel's room.

Suddenly there was a buzzing, then a flat line on the monitor. The nurse rushed toward Rachel's room, then stopped in the doorway. Tendrils of mist slowly drifted upward, and Rachel lay on her bed, her eyes closed. The golden youth and a golden girl both smiled at her.

The golden girl said, "Thank you, dear Nurse Smith." And as the mist deepened, they both disappeared.

THE HELPER

POLLY GARNET LIVED IN A TWO-ROOM
log cabin near the base of Collier Mountain. She was a
widow woman, and her only income came from the sell-
ing of two or three handmade quilts a year to city ladies in
New York or somewhere. She also bartered eggs for flour,
sugar, and other staples at the general store in the settlement. The postman always took her eggs in to Mr. Clayton, the store's proprietor, and brought the groceries back
out on his next delivery.

Polly was a stickler for neatness and believed cleanliness was next to godliness. She lived by a strict, regi-
mented schedule. She was always up at 5:30 A.M., and by
7:00 A.M. her day was well under way with every daily
chore done in proper order.

One morning dark clouds mashed against Collier
Mountain and thunder rumbled, announcing the coming
of an angry storm.

Polly hurriedly left her bed, donned her old calico
dress, and headed to the barn to take care of the cow and
chickens before the rains came. In her scurry to beat the
storm, the woman left her room before making her bed,
the first time this had happened in many years.

With the animals tended and the bucket of milk and

six eggs safely inside, daggers of lightning streaked the sky, thunder shook the ground, and rain poured like opened floodgates from the heavens.

Polly strained the fresh, frothy milk, then poured it into a gallon jug and then took it to a tiny root cellar underneath the kitchen floor. The cream always settled on the top, and later she would skim it off and churn it into butter. For now the root cellar would keep it cool, and when the storm subsided, she would take it to the springhouse for storage.

When the old woman closed the little square wooden door in the wide-plank floor, the cold wind grew in intensity, whipping tree branches about. It seemed to wail around the corners of the house to join its own echo.

A bone-chilling cold stirred somewhere inside her, and Polly hurried to fetch a shawl to ward off the growing chill. Once inside the bedroom, she saw her unmade bed with its covers all askew. She forgot the shawl and the cold and began straightening the covers, pulling the cotton flour-sack sheets tight over the feather-ticked mattress.

"I can't believe I've let my bed go this way," she said to herself. "The bed should always be made upon rising. Your mother always told you that, Polly Garnet," she scolded aloud.

It was then Polly saw the woman, vision, spirit, or perhaps ghost on the other side of the bed helping to spread the covers straight and true.

Day after day the apparition appeared and assisted as Polly made her bed, and day after day as the task was completed, the lady faded into wispy fingers of gray mist before her eyes. Polly didn't know how to respond or react to this thing or its helping her to maintain a tidy house.

After almost a week, Polly spoke forthrightly to the apparition. "Who are you? Why are you here?"

The female apparition, with her long, flowing black hair, only looked sternly at Polly and continued to pull the quilt over the fluffy down pillow.

Polly began to be afraid as she remembered her mother's and grandmother's teachings of cleanliness and everything in its proper order.

"God," she cried, "what have I done?"

In that instant the lady vanished, never to return again. Polly never, never left her room again without first making her bed. She feared something or someone from the spirit world would chide her for being lax in her daily duties as a woman of proper mountain etiquette.

WARNINGS OF MOUNT BETHYL

SOME BELIEVE THERE IS A CHURCH IN the area that doesn't always offer comfort and peace within its holy walls but harbors an unholiness, an evil. The evil threatens visitors who come to walk its floors without benefit of regular service or a man of God present.

Sarah Willis, a musically gifted young woman, lived in the rural reaches of North Georgia. She once had dreams of becoming a great pianist but abandoned her dreams when she married her high school sweetheart, Jimmy Mead. She was content to be a wife and later a mother, but as years passed, her dreams returned, especially when her daughter, Missy, displayed musical talent as well.

Long ago, Sarah's family had donated land for a church house to be built in the small, ever-growing country community where the family lived. The church was built and dedicated Mount Bethyl. Sarah, having no piano, made arrangements with the pastor to go to the church several days a week and practice. She and Missy had keys to the securely locked, heavy wooden doors, and made several trips a week to the church, which had both a piano and an organ.

On one summer afternoon, Sarah began practicing the old church hymns of her childhood. After several minutes, a strange feeling of being watched shadowed over her. She stopped her playing and looked about the sanctuary. She was alone; there was no one anywhere to be seen or heard.

Sarah began once more to caress the ivory piano keys. The feeling returned, and a voice accompanied it. "Get out of here and get out now," it said.

Sarah again stopped her playing and looked around. She even walked to the back of the church to the huge, wooden double doors to make sure she had locked them after entering.

The doors were locked, and Sarah returned to her practice. This time she seated herself behind the organ. The melody was sweet and true as she followed the notes on the old song book. As she turned the page to follow the music, however, the sensation of being watched shrouded her again. This time it was an intense heaviness. Her skin felt prickly as again the voice sounded, "Get out of here, and get out now."

Sarah immediately left, leaving the song books open to the pages she had so lovingly played. She only took time to flip the lights off and lock the doors.

She didn't tell anyone about the feeling or the voice. It was a Christian church, and who would have believed her?

Three days later, Missy and a friend went to the church to practice a duet for the next Sunday. Shortly, they returned. Missy was trembling as she extended to her mother the keys to the heavy, wooden double doors of Mount Bethyl.

"Something's wrong at the church, Mom," the girl said, her complexion pale and voice shaky. "I felt like something was watching us and then something spoke to me, but I couldn't hear it with my ears. It spoke to my mind. It said for me to get out of there and get out now."

Missy continued to hold the keys out to her mother. "I'll never go into that church again when there's not a crowd there or some kind of service going on," she said.

To this day neither Sarah nor Missy have ventured alone into the quiet of the rural country church named Mount Bethyl.

Years later, Missy needed some dates from her great-great-grandparents' gravestones in the Mount Bethyl cemetery, which was next to the church, to complete a genealogy study. In the quiet of a warm summer afternoon, Missy felt a shadow watching her. Her skin prickled and her mind readied itself for the sound of a warning, and she hurried her pace to a run as she retraced her steps from the old church cemetery before ever reaching the gravestones she sought.

Whatever had watched the girl and her mother there at the church all those many years earlier still waited and watched in the church and the resting place of their ancestors. The girl, now a woman with children of her own, remembered the eerie feeling and its warning, and she hurried to be away from the place where something unnatural lingered. She did not want to tempt whatever lingered there to anger.

Blood on the Sign

If CRUISING IN CARS WERE AN OLYMPIC sport, the young people of Pickens County would make a gold-medal team. Some of them spend more time in their cars than they do at home or in school.

Laine and her two cousins, Greg and Rick, were not only related but were good friends as well. Though they went to different schools, the cousins often got together on weekends when the brothers would come to spend time with their grandparents.

On a cool Sunday evening in early spring, the three left the small community where Laine lived with her family and headed east to the town of Jasper to spend a few hours riding around in Greg's new car.

The trio ordered hamburgers, fries, and drinks at the local Dairy Queen, then cruised town for awhile. In Jasper the kids have always had a driving route that changes as the town expands. They can drive it for hours, stopping only occasionally to talk to friends or to eat. Invariably, boredom sets in, and they stray to a few side roads.

The cousins do not remember who wanted to turn off onto quiet Nicholson Street, with its recently built houses. There is nothing ancient in the structures, though

132

in the foothills of the Blue Ridge Mountains it is impossible to say this about the land under the houses.

On Nicholson Street a yellow sign warned drivers about a dangerous curve. The cousins were just passing this sign when Laine saw something that made her scream. When she screamed, Greg, who was driving the car, put on the brakes. Once the car had stopped, he turned on the interior light, and both of the brothers saw how white her face had become, each freckle standing out.

"What is it?" Rick asked.

"Are you okay?" Greg wondered.

"Back up," Laine said.

"Why?" Greg asked.

"Back up to that sign we just passed," Laine said. "I think I saw something."

Greg looked at Rick, and both were worried. Rick nodded, and with a shrug his older brother put the car in reverse until they could once more see the sign. In the light of the headlamps the diamond-shaped yellow sign with the black arrow in a backward C looked perfectly normal to the two boys. But to the frightened girl, the sign did not look normal at all.

"Do you see that?" Laine asked them.

"See what?" the boys wondered.

"The sign," Laine said.

"Yeah. What about it?"

"Can't you see what's all over it?"

"See what?"

"On the sign. All over the sign," Laine said and pointed at the standard-issue Department of Transportation sign. "That sign is covered with blood."

Greg and Rick saw nothing out of the ordinary, but their cousin insisted. Rather than upset her more, the boys decided it would be better to take Laine home. Once there, the three told Laine's mother what had happened.

Janet, Laine's mother, was comforting. All she really cared about was seeing her daughter safe. She hoped Laine would get a good night's rest. Perhaps things would appear different in the morning.

Much to her surprise, Laine did sleep a little, but she kept dreaming about the sign and the blood staining its face. When morning came, she was still tired but got up and started getting ready for school. In the kitchen Janet was making a big country breakfast, but Laine was not hungry.

She sat down at the table with her brother and sister and turned on the radio, which was tuned to a station in a neighboring county. She was just in time to hear the local news, and after wedding and birth announcements came the deaths overnight in the county. The third one came as a shock to Laine and to Janet.

The announcer reported that a local woman had been killed in a car crash the evening before. She was going too fast on a curve on Rayford Street, and she came to rest in the opposite lane against a standard-issue yellow curve sign. She was pronounced dead at the scene.

Of course, in and of itself this announcement does not sound out of the ordinary. The fact that the woman had died at approximately the same time Laine and her two cousins were looking at the sign on Nicholson Street would not even be of note. What is strange, however, and will always haunt Laine, is the woman's name.

Although Laine is an unusual name for a female, the victim's first name was Laine. Her second was Nicholson. Laine's last name, before she married, was Rayford.

PREMONITION

EVA HUNT WAS PROUD AS PUNCH. A widow who worked at the local carpet mill, Eva had bought herself a new car. Her co-workers oohed and aahed as she showed them her first new car, a brand new 1979 red Chevy compact.

Instead of going home to an empty house after work, Eva headed out on Yellow Creek Road to her niece Chris's home. When she arrived, she was greeted with many hugs from Chris and her children. Everyone was proud for Eva.

As Eva was leaving, Chris had a worried look on her face. "Aunt Eva, I wish you would stay with us tonight," she said.

"Oh, I can't," Eva replied. "I have to go to work tomorrow."

"Please, Aunt Eva. You see, I had a dream and—"

"Oh, bosh, Chris. You and your dreams." Eva hugged Chris and the kids and left.

As Eva headed home, she laughed to herself. Chris and her dreams—she was always warning someone about something. As Eva pulled out on the main road, she admitted to herself that Chris was usually right.

Eva was just picking up speed when the gravel truck appeared in her rear-view mirror. She pulled to the right to let the mammoth vehicle pass, and when the truck caught up with Eva's car, she turned to give a quick glance. As the trailer came even with the car, it started to sway, wavering like heat rising from a tar road on a brutally hot day.

Eva slammed on the brakes as gravel and stones bounced off her little red car. The last thing she remembered was, *Why is someone throwing rocks at my new car?* Then the windshield shattered, and blackness enfolded her.

As Eva slowly regained consciousness, a stranger was peering down at her. He smiled and asked, "How do you feel, Mrs. Hunt?"

Eva knew she was in a hospital. She had an I.V. in her arm, and other tubes were running into her.

"What happened?" Eva asked. "Where am I?"

"Mrs. Hunt, I am Doctor Grant. You are in Kennesaw Hospital. You've been in an accident."

"When can I go home?" Eva asked. "I have to go to work tomorrow."

"Mrs. Hunt," Doctor Grant said, "it will be about two months before you can go back to work. You were seriously injured. Fortunately there were no broken bones, but you had a severe concussion."

"I don't care, Doctor. I can't miss work."

"Mrs. Hunt, you have been here for three weeks. You were in a coma. Your sister and niece are here. I'll let you see them for ten minutes."

Mary, Eva's sister, and Mary's daughter Chris walked over to the hospital bed.

"Oh, Mary, what am I going to do about work? And what about my new car?"

Mary said, "Don't worry. Mr. Shaw said to tell you your job is waiting for you when you're better. And the trucking company has already bought you a new red Chevy," Mary continued.

Premonition

"Oh, Chris," Eva murmured. "Maybe I should have stayed at your house. You did tell me you had a dream."

Chris took Eva's hand in hers and said, "Aunt Eva, my dream, or premonition, was that you had a terrible accident with a truck. And I dreamt that you were in a coma."

Lingering Spirits

A YOUNG MAN NAMED WILLIAM RED-
ford was stationed on the USS *Bonner*, a Navy aircraft
carrier, during part of his stay in the military. He was a
dedicated Navy man and accepted assignments without
hesitation or question.

Everyone stood watch duty at one time or another.
The duty men were assigned designated areas of the ship
and were responsible for its safety. William had watch
duty one night not long after he had reported aboard.

All was well as William patrolled his designated
areas, until he opened one particular hatch and stepped
through. The air had a deep, bone-chilling cold to it,
and he felt as if someone were watching him. The hair
prickled on the back of his neck, and he flashed his light,
completely covering the room. No one was there.

William was alone. Completing his assigned check,
he hurried through the area to the next hatch. When he
opened it and moved on to another area, the air returned
to normal, and the feeling of being watched disappeared.

A few days later William mentioned the strange feeling to one of his shipmates who had been on board the
ship for quite a while.

"Where you from?" the mate asked.

"Mountains of North Georgia," William replied, then asked, "Why do you ask?"

"Figures. Appalachian Mountains. Kindred spirits, I guess," the man mumbled.

"What do you mean?" William asked.

"Somebody else said the same thing about that offset area to the engine room a while back, but I think he was from somewhere in eastern Tennessee. You see, there was a Marine on board a few years ago. He was from somewhere in those mountains, too. Tennessee or North Carolina, I think. After the duty officer made his rounds, the Marine went in that room and killed himself. He wasn't found till the next morning. Strange," the Navy man said, "that the men from the southern mountains are the only ones who feel the cold and sense something watching them."

Word spread about the eerie feelings William had experienced and the long-past suicide of the Marine. Soon others on board began to talk of strange feelings in that area of the ship on their night watch. From then on, duty men assigned to that area of the ship went in twos, never alone, as the presence of something or someone grew stronger. All the Navy men could now feel the chill and sense something or someone watching as they made their nightly rounds.

LAUGHTER'S COLD CHILL

CLEVELAND CARPENTER, A YOUNG GEOR-
gia mountain boy, laughed as his friend Harold told him a
spooky story about a ghost that took over people's dreams
and tormented them nightly until they died or went
crazy. Buddy Falls, a mutual friend, had told the story for
truth, saying his cousin had gone out of his mind because
of the ghost and had to be committed to a hospital for
crazy people.

The two boys examined the story for untruths while
walking home at dusk, that special time of day between
day and night, when shadows take shape, then disappear
into black nothingness.

As night pushed day further behind the Appalachian
foothills and dark made its claim on the North Georgia
mountains, the boys called it a day and each went to his
home.

Soon after Cleveland had gone to bed, he yelled,
"Quit yanking the covers off me!" He reached up, pulling
the long light cord that was tied to his bed's headboard,
and the light clicked on. Cleveland was alone in the room
with the covers piled in the floor at the foot of his bed.

Righting the covers, he turned the light off. Again the
covers were yanked off. With the light again pulled on,

140

the young man searched the room for the prankster. He found no one under the bed, in the closet, or in any of the corners of the room. The door was also closed. Cleveland was alone in the room. Once again he spread the covers straight, climbed into bed, and pulled the cord, turning off the light.

Each time the light was off and darkness shrouded the room, the covers came off, even when the young man held fast with both hands.

Dawn broke. Not unlike dusk, it is that special time between night and day when shadows take shape then disappear into sunlit nothingness. It was during this time that Cleveland remembered laughing about the spooky situation told by his friend, Harold.

At the breakfast table, Cleveland told his family about fighting with the covers all night long. He said he would never again make fun of people who said they had seen or heard something that couldn't be explained.

The next night Cleveland slept soundly and his covers stayed in place, even with the dark resting heavy in his small room and the light turned off.

A Child's Lament

It is easy to lose your way in these hills. Distances are deceptive. You may walk for hours and never see another soul. Perhaps you could live for years without ever seeing another living person.

Times around here have been hard. When the Great Depression hit, many people took to the road in search of work, and most left family behind. Not far from Hinton Community, just over a few hills and to the south, a family named Lee had a piece of rocky land, and they were just scraping by. The difficult economic times of the 1930s drove John, the husband, off the land to seek employment elsewhere. He left behind Ellen, his wife, and two small children, both girls.

The children were very young, and Ellen had not yet seen her twentieth birthday. One child was about ten months old, and the other had lived but a few weeks. The young woman was fragile to begin with, and the isolation made everything she had to endure that much more difficult.

Perhaps if she'd had someone to talk to . . . but no. What she did might not have been discovered for a very long time if her husband had not returned after a fruitless month of looking for steady work.

A Child's Lament

It is said he sensed something right away. Everything was so quiet, unnaturally quiet. No babies were crying. There was no noise at all, and no movement. The man rushed into the house, afraid of what he might find. He had every reason to be afraid.

It is easy to lose your way in these hills, physically and mentally. When the man found his wife, she was alone. There were no babies. When he asked her what had happened to the children, she told them a panther had gotten both of them when she was away at the spring. He did not believe her.

The man searched the property and found nothing. Then he went to their nearest neighbor and asked if they had heard anything. The neighbor said he had heard babies crying the evening before when he was out looking for his milk cow, but he had not heard a panther. Not for years.

Soon everyone within miles had been alerted, and the search for the two children began. The sheriff came and talked to Ellen, but she continued to tell the same story. A panther had come while she was at the spring and carried the babies off. The sheriff could not believe her either.

At nightfall the searchers were ready to give up when they heard babies crying. Lanterns were brought, and everybody there followed the sound of the crying. Later they found where the sound was coming from, and presently the crying stopped. The searchers kept looking until they came to a clearing where an old oak had magnificently stood several years earlier. The tree had been reduced to a water-filled stump, and here the two little girls were found.

They were dead. According to the sheriff, who had seen death like this before, they had been dead for more than a week. The evidence pointed to murder, and as the two small bodies were lifted from the hollow stump where they had been secreted, the cause of death was obvious.

When confronted, Ellen, the mother of the two infants, admitted her guilt and begged for forgiveness. She had been lonely and afraid and knew if the babies had not been there she would have gone with her John. Only they had stood in her way, in the way of happiness. So she killed them. She took two hatpins, and where the small skulls had not yet grown together and were soft she drove the pins into their brains and killed them.

The woman did not have a trial. There was not enough left of her mind for a trial. Instead, Ellen was sent to the state facility for the insane. If she ever got out, she did not come back to these hills. John left as well, and the land reclaimed the house, taking away almost all signs of human habitation.

From the moment the bodies of the children were discovered, the stories spread. The farmer looking for his milk cow had heard the crying the evening before, but the children had already been dead. The searchers heard the crying, then found the bodies in the stump. After that, anyone who cared to pass that lonely bit of dirt road might hear the unmistakable sound of babies crying.

Just a few years ago, a man and his son were picking blackberries along that same stretch of dirt road. The father had heard the stories, but he was a God-fearing man and did not believe in ghosts. The son half wished he could hear the crying, just so he would have something to tell.

They had filled their buckets full of fat, sun-warmed berries and were about to head home when they heard something. When asked what they heard or if they saw anything, the father and son just shake their heads. They do not want to talk about it. All they'll say is, the stories are true.

144

THE STEPS OF A SHADOW

OLLIE WADDELL TOLD A STORY TO HER daughter, Mable, about strange happenings in the house of a distant cousin. The house was built somewhere around the turn of the century in the far reaches of Fannin County.

It was told that cousin Milly went to visit her sister, Edith, and planned to stay overnight. The two sisters talked to well after dark, and as night settled over the mountains and a need for sleep overtook the twosome, each went to bed. Cousin Milly was given the room with the newly ticked feather mattress on a big four-poster bed.

Milly soon settled herself on the new bedding and awaited the much-needed rest after a very tiring day.

A short time later, Milly heard footsteps in her room. Somebody or something was walking around the room. With each time around, the steps came closer to the bed.

Milly was scared for her life. She could not see anything in the darkness, but she could hear the heavy footfalls of each step. As the walking circle closed in and no more room was left for another round, something big and heavy fell across Milly lying in the big, feather-ticked four-poster bed.

Milly yelled, "Edith. Edith, light a lamp."

"Why?" came the sleepy voice from the other room. "What's wrong?"

"Hurry! Light it and get in here. Fast!" Milly cried in a fearful tone, still feeling the weight on her.

When Edith arrived with a well-lit lamp only moments later, whatever had walked the wide, wood-plank floor and fallen across Milly had vanished, leaving only a deep impression on the feather-ticked, four-poster bed.

Milly scurried from under the depressed covers and clung desperately to her sister, crying hysterically.

Even though Milly stayed in Edith's room for the rest of the night, huddled close beside her sister, she didn't sleep. Every time she closed her eyes, she heard the footsteps and felt the heavy weight across her body again.

Was it a weary passing spirit seeking rest on the newly ticked feather mattress, or perhaps a poltergeist playing impish tricks? Did whatever it was belong to the room or the new bedding, or was it connected to Edith?

Milly never knew what walked with such heavy footsteps on the old wooden floor in the black of the night. And she never knew what fell across her on the new feather-ticked bed, leaving only a big, mashed impression in the covers.

Milly never discovered answers to her questions. And she never stayed another night in her sister's house.

The Man Who Met
Santa Claus

"GRANDPA, GRANDPA, TELL US A STORY!"
cried Melissa.

"Yes, Grandpa, please," said Robert.

"Tell us a Christmas story," yelled Laura.

Delbert snarled something that no one understood,
which was just as well.

Grandpa gathered his little darlings around him, lit
his pipe, and said, "Well, I do have a Christmas story. It's
about the man who met Santa Claus. Let's call him
Harvey. Okay, kids, get comfortable.

"Well, let's see, now. Since it's Christmas 1992, it was
forty-seven years ago this very night, the night before
Christmas in 1945. Harvey was lost. There was no doubt
about that. His boots crunched in the newly fallen snow.
He shuddered in the subfreezing weather.

"When Harvey was released from the Veteran's Ad-
ministration Hospital that Christmas Eve morning, the
first thing he did was to call home. After talking to his
mama and daddy, Mary Lou, his sweetie, came on.

"'Mary Lou, I'll be home by midnight, and I have an

important question to ask you,' he said into the telephone receiver.

"'Oh, I know,' laughed Mary Lou. 'We'll be waiting.'

"Unfortunately for Harvey, he couldn't get a train from Richmond. Everyone in the world was traveling that night, December 24, 1945. Six months out of a Japanese prison camp, Harvey had regained his health—almost.

"Harvey hopped a Greyhound bus heading south, but the snowstorm stopped the bus in Columbia. Harvey started hitchhiking and after two rides found himself on a very lonely road that seemed to go on forever—to no-where.

"Despite the cold, Harvey was sweating. He staggered, almost falling into a ditch. *Darn*, he thought, *a malaria attack.* He took a quinine pill and waited.

"Harvey lurched around a bend in the road, and his feverish eyes spotted a vehicle almost off the road, obviously stuck.

"'Ho, Ho, Ho,' laughed an oddly dressed white-bearded man. 'Merry Christmas. I seem to have wandered off the road. Can you give me a hand?'

"'Sure,' said Harvey, although the vehicle he had thought was an old truck looked, well, like a sled.

"'Say, Harvey,' asked the jolly old man. 'You look a little feverish.'

"Through the haze over his eyes, Harvey said, 'I'm okay, but can you give me a lift? I have to get home.'

"'Ho, Ho, Ho, Harvey. I'll take you right to your door, just as soon as we push this here . . . er . . . vehicle back on the road. Heck, Harvey, that's why I'm here.'

"Harvey grunted and groaned, and with the help of what he guessed were eight big dogs, they got the vehicle back on the road.

"Harvey slumped next to the old man and dozed off to sleep. He heard the man laughing and shouting, 'On Dasher! On Dancer!'

"After what seemed a minute, the jolly old man was shaking Harvey. 'Harvey, wake up, son. You're home.'

"Harvey staggered out of the vehicle, the malaria attack over. He started to thank the old man, when he shouted. 'Merry Christmas, Harvey,' and handed Harvey a small package, then rode away."

"Harvey Bannister, are you telling that old story to the children? Land a goshen! You know it was an old truck," a little old woman said, entering the doorway.

"Yes, Mary Lou," smiled Grandpa Harvey.

"Come on children. I have hot chocolate in the kitchen," said Grandma.

The children screamed as one, "We like your story, Grandpa," and they ran to the kitchen with Grandma.

Harvey put down his cold pipe and reached into the drawer of the end table beside his chair. Pulling out an old box, he opened it and drew out a clay pipe, a pipe that the old man had given to him on that cold night many years ago. He packed it with tobacco and lit it. When it was warm, a small picture of Santa Claus appeared. Under it was written, *A Merry Christmas to all, and to all a good night.*

Soul Spirits

FOLKLORE AND SUPERSTITIONS IN THE rural reaches of southern Appalachia were as strong as religion and passed from generation to generation. One did not question beliefs as old as the mountains but took them as facts of life and let them be.

Twenty-one-year-old Livie Sanders was a second-grade schoolteacher in this rural area who left Appalachia when she was ten and returned eleven years later to teach, educate the young, and learn more about her own beginnings. She sprang from a place called Blood Creek some seventy miles north of Bennet, Kentucky.

The young woman had always felt she would someday return to her birthplace. She had dreams of mountains, rippling streams, forests lush and green, and a man. She had seen him in her dreams for many years, and he always aged and grew as she did. He appeared to be about two or three years older than she was with a thick mane of honey-blond hair and deep blue eyes, not unlike her own. Livie always felt a sincere kinship with the man who seemed to see into her soul, feel her joys and pains, and know her fears and loves. He was always there, somehow connected to her and to these mountains.

Livie made the seventeen-mile drive between her small rented house near the county line and the school every day. The drive was pleasant and the mountains beautiful. Spring dotted the roadsides with wild azaleas in flaming reds and shades of orange and yellow. The soft pink and white dogwood blossoms looked like suspended snowflakes amid the bright green buddings of the giant hardwoods.

Small animals scampered about the rural area in search of tender green vegetation. Birds busied themselves with the task of building nests. Livie delighted in this special time of year when the earth was renewed, except for the storms that always came with a change of weather and season.

One morning in early April, Livie was awakened by loud rumbling thunder and lightning cracking as it danced in zigzags across the black sky. Torrents of rain had begun to fall by 6:30 A.M. Livie ran fast to her old car and began her long drive to the school as the storm's darkness shrouded the land like an evil living thing spewing venom from the heavens.

Livie rounded the curves on the narrow country road at a snail's pace, and still the pounding rain limited her vision to mere inches. A flash of lightning struck a tree causing it to fall behind her, barely missing her car.

Livie was filled with fear. She began to tremble, her heart pounded in erratic rhythm, and she fell onto the steering wheel as tears streamed from her eyes. Black images of disaster whirled through her mind.

"What am I doing?" she said in a half-whisper. "Why am I out here in this cyclone? I can't go back. The road is blocked, and if another tree falls, it could kill me. Or maybe I'll just be swept off the road by this flood."

"What am I going to do?" She sobbed into her balled fist.

"Go on," a familiar voice said.

Livie turned to see the man in her dreams seated in the passenger's seat.

"What?" the young woman said, wiping her tears away to better focus her vision. "I know you," she whispered.

"Go on," he said again, then continued. "Turn left at the top of the hill."

"But that's a logging road," she stammered.

"Do what I say, and you will be safe," he said in a gentle tone.

Beginning to believe this was yet another dream, Livie did as she was bidden.

"Who are you?" she asked after making the turn.

The man was silent as he looked at the woman holding tightly to the steering wheel and watching the road closely, veering to one side then the other to dodge deep potholes and boulders. The storm lessened its fury by the time Livie pulled out onto the main road.

A man drenched to the skin flagged her to stop. "How'd you get outta there? The bridge is gone. Washed out. I just barely missed going down with it," he said in a shiver, pulling his wet coat closer around himself.

"I took the old logging road," she said in a wispy tone, knowing the strange man seated beside her had just saved her life. "Can I do anything?"

"No, ma'am," the man said. "My brother has gone for the sheriff. I'm just warning folks not to take this road."

"Then I'll be on my way," Livie responded and looked toward her passenger.

They rode in silence for a bit, and again Livie asked, "Who are you?"

"I'm your brother," came the answer.

This remark alarmed the young woman, but she wasn't afraid, just cold and shaken inside. She said, "I have only two brothers, and they are both younger, just little boys."

"I am your older brother, unborn, yet I am still your brother," he said.

Livie knew her mother had miscarried her first pregnancy. She was confused, but she knew what the man said was somehow true. She had known him all her life, yet she had never met him or seen him in the light of day. It was as if she had always felt him beside her without so much as a touch or glance.

She sighed, and he looked at her knowingly. "Where are you?" she asked with deep concern.

"I'm where I am supposed to be," he answered with a smile and slowly faded away.

Livie returned his smile and knew deep in her heart that he spoke truth. He was somewhere unknown to her, but somehow he would also always be close beside her. There was no need for a glance or a touch; they were joined in spirit and soul like these mountains and their legends, as old as time itself.

THE CEMETERY
FLOWER THIEF

GENEVA BAKERSFIELD WAS A VERY strange little old woman who lived alone in the rural community of Raven's Creek. She was known to visit the cemeteries of the community and remove flowers from certain graves. It was always the same graves: third one from the end on the south side, skipping two, then every fourth grave.

Geneva removed all flowers, artificial and real, fresh-cut or dead. No traces were left as even the fallen petals were stripped clean away.

The little woman made her journey five or six times a year, but there was never any set time. Sometimes only a few days would pass before she would return, and then again she might wait as long as three months before making her strange trek. Nobody knew why she carried on this peculiar practice or what she did with the flowers once she left the cemetery with her flour-sack bags crammed full.

Some family members of the deceased became angry and confronted Geneva. She just smiled and denied their accusations, even offering to help find the wretched flower thief.

The Cemetery Flower Thief

It is said that as soon as the families left Geneva's house, she took her faded flour sacks and went straight to the cemetery and began removing the newly placed waxed, crepe-paper poppies and plunging them deep into the sack. As she stuffed the last flower from the Gentry infant's grave into the sack, a deep voice spoke from underground, "Don't take the flowers."

The little woman looked about. There was no one in sight. She reached for some fallen crepe-paper leaves.

"Don't take the flowers!" the ground spoke again, and a nearby grave began to rumble somewhere way down low, its mounded dirt shifting and cracking like a child's sunbaked mud pies.

Geneva Bakersfield dropped the cotton flour sack and quickly ran from the cemetery as fast as her feeble legs would carry her. She never returned until some seven years later when she died and was buried third from the end on the south side of the cemetery. No flowers were present at her burial, as she requested, and to this day no flowers have ever been placed on her grave.

DEADLY DREAMS

WHEN EDDIE RETIRED FROM THE NAVY IN 1986, he moved back to Gilmer County to live in the old family place with his Aunt Emma. Eddie was a robust man, and he thrilled the local kids and kinfolk with his stories of exotic ports and countries.

It was in April that folks noticed a change in the usually happy-go-lucky Eddie. He lost interest in everything. He just sat on the front porch and stared off into the distance.

Aunt Emma proclaimed, "That Eddie had a dream, and it is worrying him silly. He should just forget it and go about his business."

As spring became summer, Eddie became more morose. His usually red face started to pale, and he lost weight. He started taking long walks and keeping more to himself. Finally Aunt Emma talked him into going to see the doctor.

Old Doc Evans had been the local practitioner for fifty years, and he knew his people better than they knew themselves. Eddie told old Doc that he was having a recurring dream, a dream that always ended the same way. Oh his—Eddie's—birthday, October 29, he would become sick and die.

"Nonsense," shouted Doc. "There ain't nothing wrong with you. I'll give you a tonic, and in a couple of weeks you'll be as good as new."

True to Doc's word, in a couple of weeks Eddie became more like his old self. He once again entertained folks with hilarious stories of life in the Navy.

However, all was still not quite right. Eddie still had his dream, and as his birthday neared, he fell silent again.

On October 28, the night before Eddie's birthday, Doc Evans came to supper at Aunt Emma's request. Eddie didn't eat much but seemed happy at the old doctor's company.

As midnight drew near and the fulfillment of what Eddie felt was sure to come, Eddie became almost resigned to his fate. When the sun rose on the morning of October 29, both Eddie and Doc were fast asleep in the parlor room chairs.

"I'll just hang around a bit today," said Doc. "That's, of course, if you don't mind?"

Eddie didn't mind at all. The two sat all day on the front porch. They talked baseball, the chances of the local high school football team, politics, and the way the world was going downhill fast, in a hand basket.

After supper they retired to the front room. They waited for the hands of the clock to move to one minute past twelve and the beginning of the new day, October 30.

Finally, after what seemed days to Eddie, the hands of the clock moved with snail-like crawling to one minute past midnight.

Eddie laughed as he shook Doc's hand. He shouted with glee, "I guess that old dream was wrong, I didn't die on my birthday after all."

Eddie's demeanor improved with every day. He regaled all who would listen with his stories, and he once again loved life. Aunt Emma was so happy that her meals soon had Eddie gaining back the weight he had lost.

On November 26 of that same year, while crossing Main Street Eddie was struck by a car driven by an out-of-state driver. The driver thought he was still on the highway, old State Road Five, and was going too fast for the small-town street.

Eddie was rushed to a big city hospital, but at one minute after twelve on November 29, Eddie died.

At Eddie's funeral old Doc Evans said, "Well, at least Eddie didn't die on his birthday. So I guess that old dream of his was wrong."

Aunt Emma, wiping the tears from her eyes, sobbed, "That dream of Eddie's was dead right. You see, November 29 was really Eddie's birthday. He lied about his date of birth when he joined the Navy. He wasn't born on October 29 but on November 29."

THE SENTINEL

IT WAS LATE, POSSIBLY EVEN MORNING already. The room was dark and quiet except for the soft hum of the air conditioner. Dan Brown lay still in his hospital bed and looked about the room. The curtain dividing the room from the hall entrance moved slightly, and he focused his eyes, trying to find the origin of the movement. There was nothing in the room, yet there was. He knew he could not explain it in words, but he knew something was there, just beyond the curtain. It was watching him. Occasionally he could see it, but not really, and could feel it, but not touch it. Once he thought he heard it, but it wasn't a voice. It was more like a thought wave or projection picked up by his mind. Maybe it was the spirit of someone who had been in this bed or this room and hadn't lived to leave, he thought. It definitely was a presence of some sort, but Dan didn't feel threatened or fearful. Perhaps, he thought again, it was a guardian angel.

A nurse entered the room. "Mr. Brown," she said, "I'm glad I don't have to wake you. I need to take your temperature and blood pressure." She busied herself with the stethoscope, then asked, "Why aren't you asleep? It's two o'clock in the morning. Our patients are usually asleep at this hour."

"I'm hurting," he answered, "and something woke me."

The nurse finished her task and charted her findings on a tablet from her pocket. Patting her patient's foot, she said, "I'll check your chart and see if you can have something for pain."

Dan watched as she quietly retreated. He listened intently for a sound. There was none. He closed his eyes, hoping the nurse would hurry back with his pain medication. He had been here eight days now—or was it nine?—he couldn't remember. But the pain was still strong, and he still couldn't move his legs. The broken ribs and pelvis and bruised kidney and lungs served as continuous reminders of how quickly carelessness could result in a life-threatening accident.

He had only been checking to see if there was any fire in the tractor's battery, but when he accidentally arced the screwdriver to the battery, it cranked and went to full throttle instantly. There was no escape in the hall of the barn, and the tractor caught his foot, pulling him down and under the large back wheel. It ran the length of his body, breaking bones and mashing and squeezing the breath from his chest as it passed over him. He remained conscious as it rolled off him and continued on toward the rambling old farmhouse. When he tried to refill his burning lungs with air, the pain gripped him like a vise, but he knew the tractor could turn and come back, and he was paralyzed to get out of its path.

"Breathe," he told himself. "Breathe short, like a pregnant woman in labor. Breathe now, or you may never breathe again."

His lungs finally inflated. He began to yell, but he knew no one could hear him over the noise of the tractor, which now pushed against his old pickup truck.

"Whistle," he told himself. There was a chance his wife could hear the high shrill over the big engine's noise.

He managed three long bursts before the pain waved over him. His wife appeared on the back steps, then began running toward him. "Call an ambulance," he yelled, trying to raise himself up on one arm. Three hours later he was here in a trauma care hospital.

The whoosh of the curtain signaled the nurse had returned with his injection. "Sorry it took me so long, Mr. Brown," she apologized, "but we're a little short-handed tonight."

She looked about the room as if feeling an unknown presence, too, but she didn't speak of it. She injected the medication, and he smiled a thank you and waited for the pain to ease. Contentment warmed the room, and before sleep could overtake him, he saluted the curtain with its rhythmic movement. "Thanks, friend," he said. "If you'll watch over me, I'll sleep now."

Silence answered the man, and he drifted off into a peaceful, healing sleep while the room's unknown sentinel stood guard.

CEMETERY PHANTOMS

WHEN PETE OLIVER WAS JUST A LITTLE boy of about eight or nine years, he lived with his mother and grandparents behind a small country church in rural southern Appalachia. During the day Pete often played in the cemetery adjoining the churchyard, imagining the gravestones to be great towers and castles. The granite and marble monuments were engraved with name, dates of birth and death, and, occasionally, some poem or Bible verses. Some were towering angels and lambs; others were just square, upright stones covered with lichen and worn almost smooth by age and the elements. Some graves were unmarked and sinking. His mother warned him to stay away from them, saying they could sink more and possibly trap him in the deep holes.

Every day was a new adventure amid this wonderful playground. At first Pete never felt any fear, and no one ever told him he should; yet when the sun began to sink behind the dark mountains, the young boy hurried for the safety of family and home. He didn't want to be alone among the dead in the dark. He didn't know why, but strange shadows loomed high and slinked around the stones when night came. What were they really? Where did they come from? What did they want? Why did Pete

162

always run away from his daytime playground when night pushed the sun from the sky?

The boy never knew exactly where the fear came from. He only knew it came from somewhere in the old church cemetery.

Plowing and planting were everyday tasks in southern Appalachia, and in the early spring Pete's grandpa, called Pap, was determined to make full use of all the daylight nature offered. He began his days early, and with the help of Dolly, the old mule, they could often plow several acres in a day, making long, straight furrows in the still, cold earth.

Pap and Dolly left the house early one crisp spring morning and began their half-mile walk to the river-bottom fields. As they passed the old cemetery, the sun rose over the top of Stover Mountain, and the old mule turned her head and rolled her eyes as if looking for something amid the aging gravestones. Maybe she saw or heard something—perhaps she just felt it—as she whinnied and picked up her pace.

"Whoa there, Dolly," the man called, calming the big animal that was hurrying to be away from the place.

Soon the sun was high. The day was warmed, and the old man and the mule plowed the fields while the boy played among the gravestones. The day grew long, and still Pap and Dolly tended the task before them and Pete was absorbed in his childhood games.

When the sun began to lay low in the sky, the boy hurried home to his mother, grandmother, and supper. It was way past dark when Pap entered the house, removing his dusty, sweat-stained hat.

"Long, hard day," he said, hanging his hat on a nail near the door and turning to wash up in the sink's basin. The water was fresh-drawn from the well, and it felt cold and refreshing to his sunburned face, hands, and arms. "Figure one more day plowing and I can plant. The ground's awful hard," the man said wearily. "Did you put corn in the feed trough, Pete?"

"Yes, Pap," the boy answered, readying himself for bed. "Mama told me. And some hay, too."

The man nodded his head in appreciation toward the boy, who was disappearing through the doorway.

Pap sat down and ate his supper, and Pete went to bed. Soon the house was dark and silent, and sleep wrapped itself around the countryside.

This night with its crescent moon did not rest. A cold wind rose from the east, and something mysterious taunted the old mule. Tired as she was from her long day's work, she made her way from the hall of the barn to the cemetery, perhaps to graze on the sweet, growing grasses or to benefit from the coolness of the gentle nighttime breeze. Once she was there, the wind quickened and something yet unexplained happened amid the rows of named gravestones, something that spooked Dolly. She began to run, and with the running a clanking rumble followed. She ran toward the house hard and fast, the rumble close behind her. It grew louder. When Dolly reached the house, she was so terrified she continued to run. With nowhere else to go, she began to run around the house. The noise followed her on the old dirt road as she slung rocks helter-skelter while she ran.

Soon the household was awake. Pete was terrified, and his mother and grandparents were startled by the commotion encircling the house. Pap quickly donned his overalls and boots, grabbed a light, and hurried to investigate.

The man caught the frightened mule, and the noise stopped. Her eyes were wild and rolling, her big red body shivering, and she snorted in fear.

Pap led the frightened animal back to the barn where he unhooked the trace chain from her bridle. He hadn't unbridled Dolly at day's end, and the clanking rumble was the chain dragging on the ground as she ran. But it was the boy who had first heard the frightening noise, and it had begun in the cemetery in the places where shadows loomed and slunk around the markers of the dead when there was no sun.

"Why did Dolly go to the cemetery in the dark?" the boy asked, shivering. "What scared her? Could it be ghosts, like the ones I sometimes see after dark?"

Nobody answered.

Now a man, the boy still lives within sight of the cemetery here in the Appalachian foothills, and to this day he wonders what enticed Dolly from the barn in the dead of night. He wonders why she went to the cemetery, and he also wonders if it was ghostly spirits and phantom shadows that scared the old mule almost to death on that long-ago spring night when he was just a boy of eight or nine years.

Visitor from the Past with Dreams of a Future

Vera Taylor, a young woman in her third trimester of pregnancy with her second child, was plagued every night by silent voices in her mind. An argument of sorts, heard only by the young woman and only in the deepest, darkest part of the night, took place while those around her slept soundly.

"Get up and make your funeral arrangements," the voice urged. "Your husband can't do it. He's going to be devastated by your death. Come on, get up and do it. You owe it to your family."

"Not now," another voice would sound. "Don't go anywhere. Go to sleep. You need rest."

The woman slept little as the voices plagued her nights. She began to fear the impending delivery of her baby, which was very near at hand, and she cried at the slightest things as her nerves and emotions were on some hellish, unseen roller coaster.

The voices became louder and more adamant with

each passing night, marking another day closer to delivery or death.

The night before Vera's due date, a voice from the dark spoke sternly, "You must make your funeral arrangements now. There is no more waiting. The time is now."

The woman threw back the covers and began to get up when the second voice sounded. "Don't," it said. "If you don't write anything down, it won't be needed. Listen carefully to me. If you put arrangements on paper, they will be put to use. Lay down and sleep."

It was a very soothing, comforting voice, and the woman lay down. Soon sleep swept her away. The next day Vera developed life-threatening problems and was admitted to the hospital, and the memory of the nighttime voices played in her mind. She was told there was a possibility of death, for her as well as for her unborn child.

"Don't write anything down and it won't be needed," she said, awaiting sleep sometime in the night in the hospital with machines monitoring her and the unborn baby.

Later, she looked to see a man standing beside her bed. He looked at her and smiled. It was her father standing straight and tall.

"Will my baby live to grow up? Will I live to see it grow to be an adult or my other baby at home?" the woman questioned as tears slid from her eyes.

There was no answer from the man, only the peaceful smiling.

"But Daddy," she said, "you're not here. You died more than five years ago."

Still the man smiled and stood beside the bed. Slowly the fear inside the woman eased, and she drifted into a restful sleep where in a dream she looked into her future. She saw herself leaving the hospital with a blanket-wrapped baby held close to her breast, her husband close behind her, and her other child close to her side. Vera woke with the assurance that all would be well in her world.

"I don't know why Daddy appeared to me," she said, "or why I later dreamed what I did. But I believe without the apparition or the dream, I would not be here today nor would my baby. I guess I needed Daddy to tell me one more time that everything would be okay. And maybe I had to see into the future just to keep the present in the proper perspective."

The Story That Could Not Be Written

FOUR MILES NORTH OF ELLIJAY, IN GIL-
mer County, Georgia, is an area known as Whitepath.
Whitepath was a legendary Native American chief who
lived in the area but was moved to the Oklahoma territory
during the infamous Trail of Tears. Along with Chief
Whitepath, thousands of Native Americans died on that
horrible journey. Before he left, according to legend, Chief
Whitepath put a curse on any future owners of his property.

While writing this book, I decided to visit the Whitepath section of the Appalachian foothills with an associ-
ate, Peggy Kendrick, and a local historian. We parked
along a deserted road and entered the so-called cursed
area.

The family who took over the property after Chief
Whitepath left built a spa and a hotel on the grounds,
and because of the mineral springs, Whitepath became a
favorite recreational area for many wealthy southern vaca-
tioners.

The historian told about the lodge and showed pictures, most with families sitting on wide verandas. The old hotel had long since burned down, and, when we entered the grounds, the only structure still standing was an arch over the entrance to the grounds.

Still feeling a dread about Whitepath, Peggy and I shuddered as we listened while the historian told of the many tragedies connected with those historic grounds. We learned that murder was a common occurrence here during the 1920s. I turned toward the spot where the lodge once stood and closed my eyes. I could hear the laughter and cheer of those long-ago guests, but in my mind I also could hear screams, screams of terrified women who knew they were about to die. Indeed, most of the victims had been women.

I cannot write the entire story of Whitepath for two reasons. First, I feel the presence of evil there like an invisible fog that seems to haunt the entire complex. Second, the historian said not all the buildings were destroyed in the fire. One building remained intact. One of the later owners had it moved to Gainesville, Georgia, where he lived. There it stayed for generations until the present owner took over. He had hired an architect to draw plans for a new Whitepath complex. It was to be a recreational area, plus an arts and crafts museum and shops from another era, and the mountain culture would be reproduced here.

I met this young man, who was in the prime of his life. He had good intentions and wanted to give something back to society. On a terrible day not long ago, while helping to load the last old building from Gainesville to take it back to Whitepath, he was struck by lightning and died instantly.

Other people can write about this historic area, but I do not feel that I am able to do it. But I just did.

EPILOGUE

THERE HAVE BEEN MANY CHANGES IN the southern Appalachian foothills since the first settlers arrived here. Most of them have occurred in the last ten years, many in the last five. The interstate highway system is the main reason for the change. The foothills now boast, or are cursed with, depending on the point of view, many new housing developments and industries, and the pristine mountains no longer supply the frontier family with food. Now the birds are startled not by a lone hunter but by the sound of a golf club driving a small ball, and by children shouting as they play in deep lakes that once supplied fish for mountain folks.

The interstates also brought shopping malls. Not too long ago folks would pack up the family and head for a larger town or city perhaps some seventy miles away—usually once a year at Christmas—or occasionally for a wedding or funeral. The rest of the time folks shopped locally, and many, if not all, had large vegetable gardens. In the autumn the womenfolk would preserve the harvest by canning or drying the fruits and vegetables. Later, the local extension services would operate canneries for the locals, doing away with much of the drudgery of home food preservation. These canneries still operate in the fall in the mountain foothills.

On Main Street or on the square, family-owned businesses sold furniture, hardware, and other necessities of life. Today most of these businesses are gone, the malls with their major department stores having tolled the death-knell for most of them. Although many older businesses have gone under, the Main Streets are thriving once again. Where the local sweet shop or furniture store once did business, now gift shops, bookstores, and computer stores have taken their place. In one section of southern Appalachia, there now are six bookstores. Two counties have built new libraries; a third plans to break ground shortly.

Many of these improvements could not have happened without an influx of new people. Many of these people dedicate countless hours to libraries, arts councils, historical societies, local hospitals, and civic organizations.

Many Appalachian people now have cable television, and their families rent movies in town to replay on their VCRs. Children—even schools—now have computers, and even dad finds ways to use the newfangled machine. Most folks still have their backyard gardens and much produce is still preserved for use when supermarket prices get too high.

Two things, though, remain the same: church and legends. Come Sunday, in scores of churches the folks celebrate God with neighbors they have known since childhood. This area isn't called the Bible Belt for nothing.

Legends bring families together as the old mountain tales are told on rainy or snowy nights somewhere in the southern Appalachian foothills. Told by grandparents or great aunts or uncles, ghost stories still hold the children spellbound as they have for generations. Who can forget the chills and goose bumps of a ghost story told by a loving relative?

Still, many worry that with computers and VCRs, many of these stories and legends will be lost forever. This would be a terrible loss for the generations yet to come. That's why even as modernization slowly works its way into rural areas, it is important that stories like these be preserved. It would be tragic if the old ways and the area's heritage were lost.